An Introduction to the Philosophy of Management

'This is a welcome, long overdue, groundbreaking textbook, at the intersection of modern organisational life with perennial philosophical debates on existence, knowledge, values, and human action.

Anchored in solid logical foundations, this book invites us on a challenging journey from epistemologies of organising to meanings of work and principles of collective action, using the work of classical and modern thinkers – such as Aristotle, Descartes, Kant, Foucault.'

Dr Cristina Neesham, Department of Management, Monash University, Melbourne, Australia

'This book is skillfully directed at invoking a wide audience to re-explore key issues such as: What is work or what can we "know" about organisational life?

The book is carefully built up by posing questions and offering deliberations from different angles – thereby activating our own processes of reflection.'

Norma R. A. Romm, Research Professor, College of Education, University of South Africa, South Africa

An Introduction to the Philosophy of Management

Paul Griseri

Los Angeles | London | New Delhi
Singapore | Washington DC

Los Angeles | London | New Delhi
Singapore | Washington DC

SAGE Publications Ltd
1 Oliver's Yard
55 City Road
London EC1Y 1SP

SAGE Publications Inc.
2455 Teller Road
Thousand Oaks, California 91320

SAGE Publications India Pvt Ltd
B 1/I 1 Mohan Cooperative Industrial Area
Mathura Road
New Delhi 110 044

SAGE Publications Asia-Pacific Pte Ltd
3 Church Street
#10-04 Samsung Hub
Singapore 049483

Editor: Kirsty Smy
Editorial assistant: Nina Smith
Production editor: Sarah Cooke
Copyeditor: Mary Dalton
Proofreader: Audrey Scriven
Indexer: Paul Griseri
Marketing manager: Alison Borg
Cover design: Francis Kenney
Typeset by: C&M Digitals (P) Ltd, Chennai, India
Printed and bound by MPG Printgroup, UK

Library of Congress Control Number: 2012944646

British Library Cataloguing in Publication data

A catalogue record for this book is available from
the British Library

MIX
Paper from
responsible sources
FSC® C018575

ISBN 978-1-44624-696-2
ISBN 978-1-44624-697-9 (pbk)

CONTENTS

ABOUT THE AUTHOR

Paul Griseri has worked in management and business education for over 25 years, and has taught philosophically related subjects to business students at all levels – from pre-undergraduate through to doctoral levels. He has a PhD in Philosophy from the University of Kent, and Postgraduate Diplomas in Management and Human Resource Management. Paul has published several books applying philosophical ideas in business contexts, and is currently the Managing Editor of the journal *Philosophy of Management*.

INTRODUCTION

WHAT KIND OF A BOOK IS AN 'INTRODUCTION' TO THE PHILOSOPHY OF MANAGEMENT?

The word 'introduction' comes from Latin roots that mean 'to lead into'. One kind of introduction is when we put together two people who have not met before – we introduce them to each other, like showing them to a room they have not been into before. Another kind of introduction is a preamble prior to engaging with the subject area in earnest: we set the scene, we give people an idea of what to expect, as if we open the door to the room to make someone ready to enter it and explore it. Yet another sense is found where a book attempts to give a summary of all the main areas of a topic. Here the introduction points to all four corners of the room, as it were, and leaves you to decide which corners, which walls and spaces, to investigate further.

This book attempts to do a bit of all of these. There is certainly an intention to lead the reader into this subject, putting them into contact with questions that they may not have considered in quite this way. Also, it aims to set expectations of how this subject matter works – the kind of mindset readers might find most useful on engaging with these ideas. Least evident is the third sense, of a general summary – it would be rash to try to provide an overview of all the different ways that philosophical ideas might apply to organisations and management, but hopefully there is an indication of some at least of the general contours of the space that this book points to. If we have not illuminated the whole room, we have at least shone a torch into some of the more important corners.

WHAT IS PHILOSOPHICAL ABOUT THE BOOK?

'Philosophy' is a word used in so many different contexts that it is easy to get the wrong idea about what this book covers. For many people, when they talk of their 'philosophy' they intend by this their general outlook, on their life maybe, or perhaps on the main purpose of the organisation they work for. Some organisations have a statement of their 'business philosophy' by which is meant roughly the purpose or mission of the organisation. It would be fair to say that this book only peripherally deals with this sense of a 'philosophy' although such statements do sometimes form the raw material of the discussion here.

Another sense of 'philosophy' is the study of our assumptions about the most general features of human existence, and the theories that people over many centuries have developed to justify or critique these assumptions. Such a practice is often associated with ancient Greece, though it also appeared independently in ancient China, India and other early civilisations, and is now associated with the academic world.

More recently some have taken the methods of academic philosophy – close attention to the use of terminology, tight arguments in which no statement is immune from questioning – and applied these directly to ordinary phenomena, outside of a theoretical context. Such philosophising of everyday life captures an important element of the original practice of the ancients, that this is meant to be an activity that integrates into people's day-to-day living, not a remote practice only carried on by a cadre of specialised experts.

This book tries to embody the spirit of this latter group, whilst adopting an approach that takes the best from the academic philosophical traditions. So there is indeed substantial discussion of academic philosophical theories, but always at the rear there is the question – what does this have to do with day-to-day organisational life? The aim therefore is to stimulate the reader to engage with *the process of philosophising*, with a view to understanding more about the assumptions that we all make in our involvement with organisations.

SO WHY SHOULD I READ THIS BOOK?

The world we live in is in great part created by managed organisations. I write something using a computer, or pen and paper – manufactured by an organisation. I buy a coffee from the local store that is part of an organisation. I send my friends emails through a network that is created, sustained and regulated by a range of organisations, both public and private. From dawn to dusk, and beyond, our lives are heavily affected by organisations and how they are managed. It is not too much of an exaggeration to say that we live in a managed world. Collectively or individually, our world is to a great extent experienced in an organisational context.

In the main, we do not question this: a sensible move in practical terms since much of the time we just have to get on with our lives. But this natural instinct does mean that our lives can be dominated and determined by assumptions that we have not fully explored.

AND WHAT IS THE BOOK ABOUT?

This book looks, not at the thinking that goes on explicitly *in* management – the justification of decisions or strategies – but rather at the thinking *behind* management. What is the basis of our understanding of what organisations are, what do we know about them, and what should they do? It is the thinking goes on before the processes of management get started, and how this might be used to justify the processes of management, that is in question here. What assumptions do we make about organisations? How are these assumptions formed, and influenced? Are they justified? We will find that answers are rather harder to come by than the questions, but the process of questioning, even if you stay with every one of your existing opinions, will deepen your understanding of what you believe and why. And thus it will deepen those beliefs themselves.

So we will here look at some – and only a selection – of the key questions that underpin organisations and management. In Section 1 the first questions will simply be about what an organisation is, and how they can be said to exist at all. We will then look at exactly what working is, and then at the idea of a leader. Following this, in Section 2 we will consider what we know about management, whether in fact we really 'know' much at all in this area, and if we do, how we are justified in claiming this. Finally in Section 3, we will look at organisational actions – how we can think of an organisation as doing something at all, what are the underlying ethical theories that can be used to justify or critique what is done in the name of organisations, and what is the significance of key ideas such as rights and responsibilities.

AND HOW SHOULD I READ THIS BOOK?

In this book you are not expected to have a detailed knowledge of business and management, though it will certainly help if you are familiar with some of the basic concepts (if you are not already). Equally, it is not necessary to have a detailed knowledge of philosophy. An interest in asking very fundamental questions and in pressing them to their limits is, though, an important attitude to adopt with the arguments of this book. What you will find is that the process of trying to answer these basic questions – of philosophising – will deepen your understanding of management, even if (as so often happens) you are not completely convinced by any of the answers you consider.

Above all the most important thing you can do is maintain a critical openness to the arguments here. As with the subject matter under consideration, so the arguments of this text are all open to question, even if you find them convincing. But with most ideas perhaps the best way to do that is to start by trying them out, as it were, see what it feels like to believe their conclusions, what they commit you to, and what they rule out. Then when you have a sense of where they could take you, you should rigorously – ruthlessly – ask why should I accept this, what if I choose to reject it? It is that dynamic that is at the heart of philosophising.

THE 'WHAT' OF MANAGEMENT

1

The first section of this book looks at three key elements of management in organisations:

- the idea of an organisation;
- the idea of work and workers;
- the idea of a leader.

The discussion will start with two distinct aims. The first is the search for clear and accurate definitions of key terms. And the second, to identify in what sense these phenomena are identified, how they come into being and how they cease – in short how they exist. However, we shall see that fulfilling these two aims depends on other issues which will only be addressed in later chapters.

A great deal of philosophical thinking is generated by defining terms and by drawing distinctions between similar ideas that are often equated. The natural source of definitions is a dictionary, however this is not necessarily watertight – dictionaries tend to tell you how words are commonly used, but not always what the word means precisely.

A definition should enable us to use a word correctly in all appropriate situations. In most cases this comes down to stating those features (the *connotation*) that capture what things are covered by the term in question (the *denotation*). If you are looking at a definition to help you understand something more fully, then it needs to tell you exactly what would be an example of the term used, and make clear how it differs from other, possibly similar terms. For example, a definition of 'profit' should cover **all** the different kinds of cases where a profit has been made, and **only** those cases – so in this case it would help you distinguish profit from a related idea such as sales revenue. In many cases the meaning of a term can be defined in terms of a combination of other, more basic terms: so for example a definition of 'airplane' might be 'a human-made structure with a long central section, two large wings and a tail, powered by engines and intended to fly'. This definition is thus composed of several constituent concepts – machine, structure, wings, flying etc.

Some concepts, however, are basic, so that it is difficult to find more fundamental ideas, in terms of which the definition may be stated. You might define a word like 'cold' as 'of low temperature' but then the definition of 'temperature' would be something like 'the degree of heat or cold' which makes the definition circular – someone who did not know what temperature was would therefore not learn what cold is.

Some very basic ideas are therefore less easily explained by other words than by showing examples – what is called *ostensive* definition. I can show people examples of cold, and if I do this enough then they will get the idea. Of course this is not a guaranteed situation. A lot of assumptions have to be made when one person decides that another person has 'got the idea', as the Austrian philosopher Ludwig Wittgenstein argued: he compared learning language ostensively to following a rule – but he also indicated how a rule may be difficult to pin down, even when one is provided with a good range of examples.[1]

But as well as the definition of very basic terms, there are many terms that have a degree of ambiguity or vagueness built into them. How do we define 'a Swedish company'? HQ in Sweden? But some companies might relocate their HQ to an offshore tax haven. Having a Swedish founder? But a company might be set up by a Swedish person in the USA. Having its main factories in Sweden? But in the present day many European companies locate their main operations in third world countries with lower labour costs. So the concept is ambiguous. We have a sense of what we want to cover but there are difficult peripheral cases that resist a watertight set of criteria that will capture all and only those cases where we would unambiguously want to say that a company is Swedish.

> A definition states what is necessary as well as what is sufficient for something to come under a certain concept. It should cover **all** and **only** those things covered by that concept.

We see in the previous paragraph an important part of the process of testing out a definition: a definition covers all cases of an idea (its denotation),

---

[1] L. Wittgenstein, *Philosophical Investigations* (Blackwell, 1953). One example of the difficulties with following a rule he used was the sequence of numbers 2,4,6,8: this might naturally lead someone to suppose that the rule was to list even numbers – but actually this sequence would look just the same, in those first cases, as a rule where once you got to 1000 you went 1004, 1008, 1012... And what would happen at 10,000? At 100,000? The point being that rules may look clear but there are often opportunities for creatively distinct ways in which they may be applied, so that one can rarely capture all those creative differences at the outset.

so given a set of terms that is supposed to define something (the purported connotation of the idea), we need to see whether it covers not just the obvious, well-known examples, but also the more unusual ones.

Sometimes we have to accept that the concept is a bit fuzzy round the edges, so to speak, and make a definition that deliberately draws a line round the most characteristic examples. This is a *stipulative* definition. So we might stipulate that being a Swedish company *just does* mean that it has its HQ in Sweden, and if there are companies excluded by this then we say that although they possess some characteristics of Swedish companies, they are not actually Swedish.

Stipulative definitions are useful where one absolutely must have a definition – say when conducting a research study. But they are less an explanation of a concept than an attempt to change the concept to something more practicable.

Another aspect of definitions is what they actually show us. A long standing philosophical question concerns the difference between *real* and *nominal* definitions. A *nominal* definition indicates the meaning of an idea as constructed from other ideas. So one can have a definition of, say, what makes something a soft drinks manufacturer, for example,[2] but one can also have nominal definitions of non-existent things, ideas simply dreamt up by someone: you could easily define what a frozen air manufacturer is, but there is no such thing (at the time of writing this).

In contrast, adherents of the idea that definition can be *real* have held that such a definition somehow captures the essence of something – to define 'company' is to show what companies actually *are*, even though these definitions may be expressed in words. To define 'soft drinks manufacturer' one needs to somehow show the underlying essence of this concept. A non-existent concept would not have a real definition, on this view.

One way to distinguish these two ideas is that a real definition would be tested out by going and looking at examples in the real world, whilst a nominal definition would be tested out by considering how people used the term in question when talking about it. In general, the majority philosophical opinion in the last century has tended towards the idea that definition is primarily nominal in nature.

One area of dispute concerning real and nominal definition has been the treatment of proper names (i.e. names that are supposed to refer specifically to one individual thing, such as 'Shakespeare' or 'Paris' or 'UNESCO'). Some would say that a proper name is really only explained by direct reference to the thing that it names – in effect a realist definition, where the

---

[2]Which presumably could be defined in terms of two more basic concepts – what makes something a soft drink, and what makes something a manufacturing company. This would then help distinguish soft drinks companies from other drinks manufacturers, say.

meaning of 'Shakespeare' is the actual person who bore that name. Many recent philosophers, construing all definition as nominal, have instead claimed that a proper name is really an abbreviation of a complex collection of descriptive terms: so the meaning of 'Shakespeare' is a set of ideas that collectively happen to pick out just that one person (rather than the meaning being the individual person with that name). One conclusion of this is that in different circumstances a different individual (or even more than one individual) might possess that collection of descriptions – Shakespeare could have been a different person, in effect. However, this has not closed the debate; one very influential contemporary philosopher, Saul Kripke, has argued that some definitions of proper names are 'real' in that they connect directly with the thing so named – he calls these names *rigid designators* (so 'Shakespeare' would, in any conceivable situation, refer to that specific person). This argument is relevant in this section of the book when we consider definitions of 'organisation' and what these and related terms really tell us.

We see here that even a simple matter such as defining a term can conceal significant and substantial issues. And yet we need decent definitions of ideas in order to discover more about what organisations are, what are the consequences of calling something an organisation as opposed to saying it is not one, and so on. Throughout not just this first section, but also right across the book, we will find that key arguments turn on questions of just what we mean by a certain term, so definitions matter.

WHAT ARE ORGANISATIONS?

1

When you have read this chapter, you will be able to:

- analyse and critique definitions of organisation
- evaluate potential conditions for an organisation to be said to exist.

DEFINING 'ORGANISATION' IN TERMS OF MEMBERSHIP

1.1 The most fundamental question in any philosophical enquiry into organisations and management is: what exactly is an organisation? We can distinguish the two following senses of this question:

What is it for something in general to be an organisation?
How can we decide whether a specific 'thing' is an organisation or not?

Although the two questions are clearly related, it may be possible to answer the first and not be able to answer the second. I may accept that an organisation possesses features *a, b, c, d,* but not be able to find out whether some particular collection of people has all of these features. Or I may see features *a, b, c* and *d* all present, but not be sure that they all attach to the same identified entity.

When we talk about an organisation, it goes beyond the physical manifestations – we do not mean just the buildings, or the people. Take away the buildings and you have an operational problem – but the organisation has not ceased to exist. Take away the people, leaving the rest, and you have a bigger problem, but arguably there is still an organisation there, something waiting to be re-populated. The 'organisation' is somehow abstracted from its people and its buildings – just as it would be from the machinery, the legal documents, the goods and services it produces and delivers. It 'exists' – but we do not seem to be able to explain how in terms of its components. Each of the things mentioned above are part of something being an organisation, but no specific cluster of them represents 'the' organisation. None is necessary, and none on its own is sufficient – even a set of legal documents defining a company is not enough for us to say that an organisation exists. Some cluster of these elements must be sufficient for us to say that an organisation exists, but it is difficult to pin down exactly which.

Let us start by looking at a couple of 'standard' definitions of an organisation, as given in Box 1.1.

BOX 1.1

DEFINITIONS OF 'ORGANISATION'

Business Dictionary (online)
A social unit of people, systematically structured and managed to meet a need or to pursue collective goals on a continuing basis.
Oxford English Dictionary
An organized group of people with a particular purpose, such as a business or government department

---

As this indicates, one well known attempt at a definition of an organisation is that it is a collection of individuals somehow associated with the achievement of certain goals. The first example of this kind of definition makes clear that these are somehow 'collective'. One would presume that this indicates that they are commonly agreed amongst that group of people. But this on its own is not enough – a group of protesters demonstrating in the street will often have a set of commonly agreed goals, but they will not comprise an organisation.

Both of the definitions given above also include some aspect of control – in one the idea of the group being 'systematically structured' and in the other of being 'organised'. But again our protesters might be systematically structured – one group is set up to go to the palace, and another to the government buildings – without that making them an organisation. Some definitions of 'organisation' include the idea of being self-consciously structured and purposive, but again a group of protesters might be fully aware of what they are doing, how and why, without this making them an organisation.

We might turn this around and ask what are the differences between a collection of people such as a group of protesters, and an organisation? One presumably is that there is a formal process of including someone in an organisation – it possesses *recognised members*, which the protesters would generally not have. Another might be that it is has a *degree of longevity* that a group of protesters would not have, these having come together often almost spontaneously for a specific and defined event.

So perhaps our definition could become:

> An ongoing group of individuals who are formally recognised as associated with the group, and with a common set of goals which they are systematically structured to accomplish

Is this enough? Well, the standard turn in philosophical discussion is to see if we can construct a *counter-example* – here this would be either a case that we would all agree is an organisation but lacks some aspect of this definition, or one that we would all agree is *not* an organisation but has all of these features (in fact we already did the latter when discussing the previous purported definition, by looking at the example of groups of protesters). If that attempt fails then we might feel justified in accepting this as a definition, provisionally at least.

Now consider this case: a number of customers of a retail computer company have been asked by a PR company to form a users' group for the company. They regularly visit an online forum, where they express their views, give feedback, swap explanations of how to deal with certain problems, etc. They have to register online with a password and user name in order to be able to read or write to the forum. They participate because they all want to improve the services of the company. And they are clear that their role has a place in the structure of how the company gains feedback from their customers. Are they an organisation in their own right?

It is not clear how we should answer this. The collection fits the purported definition given above. The individuals have an ongoing relationship, they have some kind of formal association, they have a commonality in their goals, and there is a structure to their contributions. But do these individuals regard *themselves* as part of an organisation? Some might but it is just as possible that some might not – indeed it is not impossible that *none* of them thought this.

Such an 'organisation', where no one thinks that they are members, would seem to be a weird kind of set-up, almost an illusion or a deception, and runs counter to what people generally seem to say about organisations. The *recognition* of the organisation's existence seems to be a key part of the idea. So it seems that a further part of something being an organisation is that it is somehow or other perceived by members or others as a unit, an entity.

Around this point some readers may be feeling impatient. Why do we need to spend so much time worrying over definitions? We all know what an organisation is – look at the examples: Tata Motors, Goldman Sachs, Amazon, the Australian Government, the International Monetary Fund, Amnesty International, FIFA and so on. It is pretty clear to most people that these are organisations, so if we cannot give a watertight definition does that matter?

It may matter more than appears at first sight. If we cannot give a clear definition then we will not know how to deal with new cases. Today some organisations have very small physical manifestations, being mainly organised around internet networks. If I have a problem with a particular organisation, where do I go for redress? If there is a building then it is clear where I go. But some organisations nowadays are what are called 'shell' companies, with no physical office, and perhaps just a website to indicate their presence to me. Similarly, in so-called group structures, where there is a holding company and a number of subsidiaries, it is often extremely difficult to sort out which is the 'real' company from a legal pyramid of cross-holdings and so-called 'paper' companies. So what exactly is 'the' organisation can in some cases become confusing, even though in many other cases (e.g. a small store in our local area) we can see and know clearly that it is an organisation. Furthermore, as we have indicated above, some collections of people may form quickly and without the supporting manifestations of offices, legal contracts etc. that we usually look to as signs of an organisation.

DEFINITIONS IN TERMS OF AGREEMENT

1.2 So we see that there are problems with the membership aspects of standard definitions. There are further issues with what counts as 'agreed' or 'common' goals, as well as with who exactly are the people who might be counted as 'members' of an organisation.

Consider what makes something an *agreed* goal of an organisation. Does this mean that everyone in the organisation agrees to it? Hardly – it is well known that many employees do not share the official goals of their organisation. So is it a *majority* accord that is necessary? One problem with this is that we might not actually know what proportion of the workforce agrees with the official goals of the company: people often do not admit to their doubts over corporate goals, in case this might adversely affect their position in the organisation. Another is that it would seem odd to say that one group of people with, say 51 percent agreement, with goals, is an organisation, whilst another, with say 48 percent agreement, is not. And whatever percentage one specified, a similar argument would apply.

So is agreement with corporate goals not necessary at all for something to be an organisation? Remember that here we are trying to understand what it is for something to be an organisation at all, not whether an organisation is well run, or healthy, or effective. Consider the opposite case: suppose there were a collection of people, systematically structured in their activity, where *no one* actually agreed with corporate goals. It might be unusual but it would seem plausible to say it is an organisation – perhaps someone once set the organisation up with certain goals in mind, set these out in a codified form, and no one has ever questioned these, even though no one now really accepts them.

So it looks like 'common' goals in our definition of an organisation is not exactly the same as 'agreed' goals. But we would presumably still want to have some sense in which the goals that people are working towards have some connection. A group of individuals, however systematic in their behaviour, who are working towards completely different goals is not an organisation in the sense of an economically or socially relevant collective activity. So we presumably will need to include in our definition some idea that people are working towards similar or common goals. Exactly how many people, and exactly how similar, may be difficult to establish. That a few people are working against corporate goals would not mean that the collective was not an organisation. And in many cases there may not be an exact identity between people's understanding of what the corporate goals are. Various departments in an organisation will often have their own slant on what is being done – the marketing department of a car manufacturer may talk of meeting the customers' needs for new and reliable vehicles, whilst the HR department may talk of enabling staff to have the right skills and rewards for the efficient production of cars. Producing cars is central here, so variations between different departments' or individuals' understanding of this may not matter.

However, a couple of unusual cases may clarify this aspect of our definition. Firstly, consider a group of scientific experts, called together by their government to work on a certain project; in reality the government wants to spy on them to see if any of them are likely to reveal state secrets to a foreign power. Now, here there is a structure, and there are common goals. But these goals are not the reason why the 'organisation' was set up. This seems to be on the fringes of what we might regard as a genuine organisation – we might say that it was an organisation with deceptive official goals. Now change this example a little – each expert is told a different story about the project, so that each of them has a different understanding of what it is about, and is instructed that under no circumstances must they reveal this to any of their fellow project workers. So we have a whole collection of people, working in a structured way, but all with a different idea of what they are doing.[3] Again this is odd, but probably we would still say that it is an organisation – the scientists are working in a concerted way towards a goal, though it is not actually one that any of them knows about, still less accepts.

So maybe we can discard the idea of commonly agreed or shared goals. What is important is not whether the members of the organisation share or agree the goals, so much as that there is some goal towards which all are in some way working, even if they do not actually know what that is. So 'common' goal

---

[3]Perhaps this is less far fetched than it might at first sight seem. Governments, especially when they are developing military technology, may not wish to entrust their scientists with the knowledge of what is being done, in case one of them might violate security and reveal the nature of the project to outsiders.

for the purposes of our definition is not the same as 'commonly understood'. It need not carry any sense of someone being aware of the real object of the organisation.

Now let us look at yet another similar case. Consider a similar group of scientific experts who are asked to work on a project, but are not told that they are doing so. Each may be asked to work on a specific task, without being informed that it is intended to fit in with what others are doing. Here they may still be working in a systematic way towards a goal that someone at least has in mind, but lack any sense that they are working together. As far as they are concerned they are dealing with one specific task that has no bearing on what anyone else is doing. True, they might suspect that there is some further value to what they are doing – after all, nothing is much use in isolation – but as far as they know there is no co-ordinated collective activity or end to which they are contributing. Some government research establishments may well work like this – investigating a range of different things, one or more of which some official hopes may lead to a valuable result, but of which the scientists are unaware, and without any formal link between what each researcher is doing. In such cases it may not even be that their activities can in fact be co-ordinated – it might require an investigation to determine whether this process or that can fit together at all – but what would count is that someone at least hopes or expects that they might. It is probably a matter for each reader to read this and consider for themselves whether or not this would be justifiably considered as an organisation – but it is at least plausible to say so.

Now consider a more extreme version of this example, where the scientists happen to be working somewhere, on things that *some external individual* thinks might lead to some useful result. Perhaps a criminal mastermind is observing the work of a variety of scientists, perhaps even subtly influencing what they do, in the belief that if this scientist achieves result x and this other scientist achieves result y, and so on, then s/he, the mastermind, can use the knowledge gained to construct some deadly weapon. It seems less plausible to consider this as an organisation. It would be incidental to the formal activity of the scientists that any co-ordinated result came about, even though some-one – the criminal mastermind – was actively trying to make this happen. In the earlier case the scientists might be aware, in some vague sense, that some co-ordination of their work might take place, even though it was not part of their detailed understanding exactly what or who was doing it, whereas in this case it seems that such co-ordination is the specific intention of no one directly formally associated with the activity of the scientists.

So, our discussion of these various hypothetical cases seems to have established the following:

- Physical manifestations of an organisation are not necessary elements of an organisation.
- Members or participants of the organisation need not be aware of the common goal.

- Someone formally associated with the organisation needs to have a goal that relates to the activity of the collective.
- The activities of members/participants need by and large to be co-ordinated, or to have the possibility of being co-ordinated.

What is interesting about these points is that they do not actually refute the two definitions given in Box 1.1. They do place them in context, clarifying especially the ideas of collective goals and of co-ordination. The arguments on which they are based do, however, turn on our instinctive, intuitive ideas about what we would be prepared to call an organisation, and someone might simply challenge such intuitive responses. Certainly, at some points the decision as to whether a case was one of an organisation or not, seemed to be if not arbitrary at least rather close.

Maybe, however, we are searching for too much. Up until now we have been trying to answer both of the questions we stated at the start of this chapter; not only what we mean by the idea of an organisation but also how we would decide in any particular case that something was or was not an organisation. The Austrian philosopher Wittgenstein suggested that we understand meaning differently. He said that the totality of examples of a word or term is not always exhaustively set by an existing explanation of its meaning – this is one of the consequences of his argument about not being able to predict a whole series of steps when following a rule after being given a series of examples. He said instead that when faced with a fresh case that raised a question of whether it might count as an example of the term or not, we would make decisions based on a range of features. Each new example that we accepted would have a *family resemblance* to other examples already accepted, but there would not necessarily be a specific set of properties that they absolutely had to have. In our case, we might say that the family resemblances would cluster around ideas of collective activity, of co-ordination, of a collective outcome or purpose. But arguably the examples we have encountered suggest that there is no specific interpretation of these that is the determining factor in whether or not something is an organisation.

HOW DO ORGANISATIONS EXIST?

1.3 At this stage we will move away from the issue of defining an organisation (not that we have settled the matter) and look at the other question we posed ourselves in this section: in what way would we say that an organisation exists? When does one come into being, and when would it cease? When can we say that there is one organisation or many present in a situation?

We can see that our discussion of *definitions* helps us to understand some of the issues about the *existence* or otherwise of organisations. We could say that an organisation exists when some of those features identified in what we called the standard definition are present. But this is easier said than achieved. For one thing, we have argued that whilst some aspect of co-ordinated objective is involved, it does not seem to be connected directly with the conscious intentions of any individual. So it would be difficult in some of our more extreme examples to detect whether there really was an organisation present or not – in some cases there may be a collection of people without anyone consciously having a structured plan as to what they are doing, and yet their behaviour looks very similar to another group where in fact someone did have such an intention. Box 1.2 indicates a puzzling example of this issue.

BOX 1.2

THE SHORT LIFE OF AN ORGANISATION

The High Fields Arts Collective was the idea of Johan Roers, a retired theatre manager. He realised that in his local rural community there were several people who had some connection with the performing arts. He contacted 16 people and suggested that they form an amateur arts group serving the community. Several were interested in such a move, although they mostly expressed some kind of reservation: one said that they would be ready to support the initiative so long as there were sufficient other supporters with professional experience, to ensure that it was of a good standard.

Mr Roers felt that this was good encouragement, and wrote a short business plan, sought and obtained a small degree of funding from the local council, hired a space for rehearsals and with an office, printed leaf-lets and notified local media. An inaugural meeting was set for a specific date and Mr Roers contacted everyone who had expressed some interest, inviting them to this.

No one arrived for that meeting. When Mr Roers contacted each of the invitiees, the message was the same – they thought it was a good idea but wanted to see how much interest there was before they would make a com-mitment to joining. Regretfully, Mr Roers cancelled the room hire and returned the council grant. No more was heard of the High Fields Arts Collective.

Did this organisation exist at all? If so, for how long? If not, what did it lack?

There are however further potential problems with the existence of an organisation. Generally speaking if one can talk about an 'it' one should be able to identify an example. Now in one sense this is very clear – we can give lots of examples of organisations. But could we point to one? I can point to the offices of, say, Citibank. I can even point to its head office. But is this the same as pointing to *the organisation itself*? Suppose Citibank changed its head office, or decided to have just virtual offices; it is still the same organisation. So the physical presence of a building does not constitute its existence. And similarly with its staff – no one individual or group of individuals comprises the organisation: if the organisation changes its people it does not change into a different organisation, it is the same business but simply with different workers.

As we saw earlier, similar things could be said of its legal documents. But Citibank exists, in a way that Lehman Brothers does not (these days).

Lehman Brothers is an interesting example of a former organisation. It clearly once upon a time existed: people traded with it, worked for it, lent it money or borrowed from it, and yet at a certain point it began to cease to exist. However, at the time of writing (summer 2011) the organisation has not entirely disappeared – there is an operation called Lehman Brothers Holdings which is carrying out tasks such as preparing to deal with creditor demands, etc. So even bankruptcy is not exactly the final moment in the existence of an organisation; there are various legal moves that need to be finalised before a firm completely disappears, and in some cases a company may be rescued during those final days or weeks, say if some investment 'angel' comes along and decides to bale out the bankrupt company. This has happened several times with sports clubs, which have loyal followers but on several occasions have come close to being shut down. And even when an 'angel' does not come to the rescue of a company, it may have residual obligations, and even funds, that require something to persist for some time to come. Where one organisation ends and another begins may be difficult to easily indicate. For example, upon the closure of the Greater London Council (GLC) in the UK in 1988, an organisation called the London Residuary Body took over some of the remaining funds of the GLC and administered some of its services, even employing some of the GLC staff, and using its premises. How different is this from the situation where a government official continues to administer the finances of a company, paying tax, bank loans, and obligations to shareholders? In the first case it is clear that one organisation has ceased to exist and another has taken over some of its activities. In the second it looks more as if one organisation is being slowly wound down, so it is in the process of ceasing to exist, even though it has not finally 'died'.

The position can become more fuzzy still – suppose a company whose name is a well known brand goes into bankruptcy, and then as it finally is disappearing an entrepreneur comes along, buys up the brand name and carries on producing and selling the product in exactly the same way as it had been produced before, under the old company name. Has the old organisation continued, albeit with a brief interruption, or is it a new organisation that happens to look very similar to one that existed before?

HOW DO ORGANISATIONS COME INTO BEING?

1.4 If we look at the other end of the life of an organisation – when it comes into being – there are parallel areas of uncertainty. Clearly there are some points at which we can definitely say that an organisation exists, for example when it has been constituted by legal deed. However, although that may mark the beginning of the legal existence of an organisation, it is clear that it may have already existed for some time already, outside of a legal definition in effect.

Suppose two people start doing something together, working out a systematic division of activity between them, with a common purpose. Has an organisation come into being? If they intend to carry on then one might be tempted to say that it has. Suppose, though, that the two people do not intend to work together for more than one event (perhaps they are organising a street party for example) and yet afterwards they decide they will – when did an organisation come into being? When they decided to carry on working, or when they started working together originally? Either answer seems plausible. If we were to say that it was when they first started working together, this would have the odd conclusion that some such 'organisations' come into being and then pass away without anyone ever noticing this – when, say, these two people started organising a street party together but never decided to do anything else. On the other hand, if we say that an organisation exists when two people decide that they will work together on an ongoing basis that would seem to suggest that the critical feature is someone's *intention* to work collectively. But what if one person of the two decides that they want to do this and the other does not, and then eventually the first person persuades the second to work together – did the organisation come into being at that time or at the earlier time when someone first thought of this?

In practical terms it may not look as if an answer to this matters, but it is extreme and unusual cases like this that probe our understanding of what we mean by talking of an organisation existing. Certainly there are many anecdotes of successful visionary entrepreneurs who had an idea and then had to persist in overcoming opposition and apathy before anyone took them seriously. Suppose one of these had a clear idea of what they wanted to do, and how the organisation that they wanted to set up would operate. Do we identify the beginning of the organisation as the point at which someone else agrees to work with the entrepreneur, even though the entrepreneur already has a clear picture of how the organisation will work? Look back at Box 1.2 – it is tempting to say that there never was an organisation in this case, but presumably if just one person had turned up to the inaugural meeting we would probably conclude that the organisation did in fact exist.

Related to this is the question of whether there can be such a thing as a single-person organisation. A two-person organisation where one person leaves is presumably still an organisation, and there are after all many one-person companies. So if our entrepreneur decides that s/he will run a business in such and such a way, even though later on they will need other people to help them, once they have thought of this then it would seem that we have to agree that an organisation has already come into being. But what about bright ideas of this kind that never reach the light of day? Are these organisations that never started, organisations that started in someone's mind but never got any further, or are they not organisations at all unless they eventually gained some kind of physical manifestation? The latter, though reasonable, would make it possible that two people might have exactly the same idea, with the same conception of how to operationalise it, and yet one of these is the beginning of an organisation (because it does eventually turn into a real organisation) whilst the other is not (because it never goes any further).

Puzzles also appear with the idea of how we identify or individuate organisations. The typical modern multinational company is in reality a cluster of legally separate companies, for example each national subsidiary may have a distinct legal status, the 'only' connection being that a holding company back in the home country owns a controlling share in the subsidiary. Some conglomerate corporations own companies that they have no intention of absorbing into their main operations, and hold others that they are trying to fully merge into the main firm. One or many organisations? This is indeed a practical issue as we need to know exactly who is finally accountable for the actions of a subsidiary, and there have been cases where a holding company has avoided being taken to task for illegal or unethical behaviour specifically because they deny direct responsibility for a subsidiary's actions.

Further, when one person starts working with someone else, and then decides to do something separately, when is this a different organisation? A famous example concerns the social networking company Facebook – the originator of this, Mark Zuckerberg, was associated with three co-students who later claimed that Zuckerberg had agreed to work with them on developing their version of a social networking website.[4] Whatever the specifics of this particular case, it is clear that in some cases we might regard someone as working as part of an organisation by assenting to do so, and therefore whatever is so developed could in principle be regarded as the property of the original 'organisation'.

These examples indicate that especially in the case of business start-ups, where there is often a degree of fluidity about what is being done and on

---

[4]Which they called HarvardConnection.com. The three co-students were Cameron Winklevoss, Tyler Winklevoss, and Divya Narendra. The story was dramatised in the movie *The Social Network*.

whose behalf, the question of what organisation, and how many of these, has come into existence may become a substantial matter. Our discussion seems to indicate that at least sometimes someone's *intentions and beliefs* may be an important element in whether or not an organisation exists, or has come into being. But as we have seen, the presence of an intention does not seem to be a necessary condition of an organisation existing, and in some cases may not even be sufficient.

THE SUBSTANCE OF AN ORGANISATION

1.5 Of course these puzzles only appear because we are trying to pin down exactly what an organisation is. They need not create serious problems for a professional manager or entrepreneur, but they do underline that the concept of 'organisation' is not easily explained with absolute precision.

One of the most celebrated discussions of existence is to be found in the work of Aristotle[5] where he explains that although we can use the idea of existence in many different ways, these all stem from a fundamental sense, in which something is what he calls a *substance*. This is not to be identified with anything material, but is related to the *essence* of something, what something is at root (what makes something an organisation at all) as opposed to accidental features it may have (this organisation is large, that one is small etc.). Essence is what something is by definition. Although Aristotle's views are difficult to clarify, and commentators differ strongly about what he actually meant, we can summarise his view as being that the essence of something is related not to its material content but to its *form*. We could therefore infer from this that the essence of an organisation is not the bricks, or the people, but the means in which these are combined.

Without being committed to a full acceptance of Aristotle's ideas, we might draw on this idea and construct an interpretation of an organisation as a certain kind of form. Organisations have to have physical manifestations, just as a statue needs to be made of something. As we have seen, the essence of the organisation is not bricks, people, or documents etc., but some other underlying feature. We have not entirely clarified this, but arising out of the many puzzles we have identified there seems to be a core sense of an organisation as being related to *the intentions* of individuals to work to achieve certain outcomes or purposes. The puzzles we encountered mainly stem from treating an organisation as rather like an object,

---

[5]Aristotle, *Metaphysics*, Book Zeta.

with specific boundaries in space and time (when does it start? where is it? and where does it stop?). Once we focus on the essence of an organisation relating to intentions then these go away, for this makes the essence of an organisation more of an idea than an object, and ideas do not have beginnings and endings, or insides and outsides. Note that we said 'more of' – organisations would not be purely ideas: they have physical aspects, such as the people, documents, buildings etc. referred to previously. But following Aristotle's style of thinking, we might say that these are accidental aspects, and the underlying reality of an organisation is its idea.

Where have we got to in this discussion, then? We have seen that there are many puzzles if we regard an organisation as basically a kind of object. An Aristotelian kind of account, one that identifies the essence or form of an organisation as related to its intention, ducks these problems. This is not, though, to suggest that such an account is absent from its own problems. As we have seen – whose intention? And also when do these intentions come into play? Several of the puzzles previously considered come into play all over again, and other fresh ones may also become apparent (e.g. how to account for changes in the intentions of key individuals within the organisation). However, we have seen enough to recognise some at least of the issues involved in considering how an organisation may be said to exist.

The key lessons we have learnt from this chapter are:

- The definition of what it is for something to be called an organisation appears to rest on the idea of an intention.
- The existence of an organisation also involves reference to intentions though there are problems with this.
- An approach such as Aristotelianism provides partial answers to these issues, though in doing so they tend to make clearer the problems, rather than provide definitive final answers.

In the next chapter we will again try to establish definitions – in that case, looking at what work is.

QUESTIONS FOR REFLECTION

1 If two people decide to form an organisation, but then never do anything about it, has an organisation ever existed? If so, how long does it exist for? If not, what needs to happen for us to say it has come into being?

2 In what circumstances could you have a fake organisation – one that someone makes out exists when it does not at all? What if someone is fooled by this and genuinely starts 'working' for this fake organisation?

FURTHER READING

There is a massive literature on Aristotle's metaphysics. Interested readers are advised to start with an introduction such as the *Routledge Philosophy Guidebook to Aristotle and the "Metaphysics"*, by V. Politis (Routledge, 2004).

An interesting alternative view of criminality and organisation (a topic which will be referred to again in the next chapter) may be found in *Alternative Business: Outlaws, Crime and Culture* by M. Parker (Routledge, 2011)

WORKERS AND WORK

2

When you have completed this chapter you will be able to:

- critically evaluate definitions of 'work' and 'workers'.

In the previous chapter we tried to define a key term, but encountered cases that defied our attempts. Granted, these were relatively unusual, but all the same they indicated that the most basic idea of an organisation is not quite as clear as we might like it to be.

In this chapter we are turning our attention to another central idea in understanding organisations and management – that of the worker. We will start with an attempt to define work and working that has some similarity in approach to that adopted in Chapter 1. We will, though, spend less time on this activity, not because it is less important, but because once we have seen how the process of philosophically critiquing definitions works, it can be assumed that the same processes will operate here too. Once we have looked at the issues of definition, we will look at the problems relating to the significance, and to a lesser extent the ethics, of work, and what it means to be a worker, to have work, and to carry out the activity of working. This will then feed into the question of how far working is a part of human nature.

DEFINING WORK

2.1 We shall start with a core example of a worker. By 'work' here we mean more than just activity – it is about the relationship between those who carry out activity and the organisation for which the activity is performed.

Working is often seen as *transactional*. That is, that someone does something in return for something else. Suppose someone is paid by a company to carry out certain tasks for a specific time each week. One potential definition therefore might be:

A worker is someone who performs specific tasks for a reward

On its own this is not quite right, as it would cover someone picking up a lost wallet and keeping the money in it. Perhaps we can strengthen this by adding the sense in which something is part of a contract:

> A worker is someone who performs agreed tasks for an agreed and speci-fied reward

Although there are still some holes with this (a child agreeing to tidy his or her room in return for a treat would fit this definition) we will treat it as a fair place to start. Now, there are some activities which we might not normally consider as 'work' that fall within this definition: criminal activity such as fraud or theft, for example. But we might be prepared to accept this conse-quence, for even though such behaviour may be illegal (and in many if not all cases also immoral) nevertheless it has similarities with more orthodox work – for example someone may do it as a permanent source of income, there can be organised groups of people doing it, there are leaders, the activity may be structured, and it may be rewarded on fixed or performance-related bases.

How about voluntary work? Here there is no economic reward, by defi-nition. But we could say that a voluntary worker derives some personal sense of satisfaction by performing tasks, and this therefore provides a form of reward. Once we allow this, however, there are other cases that seem less plausibly regarded as work. Take simply carrying out tasks for a friend: if I agree to help out my neighbour clearing their garden, that clearly is not 'work' in the sense we intend, even though I might perform quite a lot of activity in doing so, and gain a personal feeling of satisfaction at helping my neighbour. We cannot exclude this kind of example by requiring that some-one carry out tasks for an organisation, since some people who are clearly employed and working (chauffeurs, maids, butlers) may do so not for an organisation but for an individual.

Perhaps we might however focus on the idea that work is a *relationship* between parties where one performs set tasks for the other party in order to derive a specific reward. This can also include the self-employed, since in this case they still provide services, but to clients rather than to an employer. So what kind of relationship is involved? In Chapter 1 we identified some aspect of *intention to work together* as being crucial for us to call a working arrange-ment an organisation. In parallel maybe we could consider that the key fea-ture of the working relationship is an intention, in some way shared between the two parties, that some task is done in return for some kind of reward.

Again, however, voluntary work creates a difficulty. Whilst someone run-ning an organisation can presume that the voluntary worker gets *some* kind of reward for making their contribution, it may not be clear exactly *what* the reward is. People carry out voluntary work for many reasons – in the case of charitable work, it might be done out of a moral sense of imperative, or for social contact, or even as a relief from the stresses and strains of some different but demanding employment. Although it can be guessed that some reward is sought by the person carrying out the voluntary work, it may not be clear – even to the voluntary worker her- or himself – exactly which reward is involved. Whilst this does not undermine the idea that voluntary activity is a kind of work, it does seem to make it strange to say that a key aspect of this relationship is an *intention*. Whilst it may be clear that there is an intention to carry out a set of tasks or activities, it is difficult to say exactly what the worker receives in return. And if one claimed here that the intention was for someone to carry out specific tasks in return for unspecified rewards, it would make voluntary working odder than it ought to be.

Voluntary work creates further difficulties for this transactional conception of work. In formal employment there is an explicit agreement that if a worker does x, y, z then they will in normal circumstances receive economic rewards a, b, c. With a voluntary worker there is an agreement that they will do x, y and z, and it is anticipated that they will receive some kind of reward, even though we might not in some cases be able to state exactly what the reward might be. But suppose that the voluntary worker is working for a charity that he or she believes is providing support for poor people in a rural region. Suppose now that after a while they realise that the money is all going into the coffers of a dictator in that region. They may feel betrayed, and they may indeed decide not to work for that specific voluntary organisation again. But does that mean that what they had been doing was not work? Surely not; they worked on a voluntary basis, and then when they saw the situation they decided not to continue working because they were not getting the sense of moral contribution that was their reward for working. So the *actual presence* of a reward is not necessary for something to count as work, if we are to continue to maintain that someone doing something on a voluntary, unpaid, basis is still a worker. An *anticipation* of reward would seem to be all that is necessary to make someone a worker, in this conception.

Anticipated rewards also apply in formal paid employment, in that although a standard wage or salary is usually agreed in advance of someone undertaking employment, there are countless cases where unforeseen changes in working practices mean that someone is expected to vary their actual behaviour, replacing tasks or changing hours of work. Sometimes there are disputes between employee and employer over the reward for these changes in tasks (for example extra allowances for working night shifts) but no one disputes that it was after all work. Indeed, it is often claimed by employers in disputes that some of the reward for employment is not financial: especially in the cases of human service occupations such as nursing or teaching, the sense of contribution to people's development or well-being is often seen as an important element in the reward that workers *anticipate* that they will derive, over and above such financial rewards as they gain. Whether or not they do actually get this sense of reward does not, though, detract from the fact that they have carried out work.

There is a further puzzle with this transactional model. If I do work for someone else with the anticipation of getting some kind of reward in return, a certain freedom is implied in this choice, but it also implies that the party making the choice has sufficient information. In the light of our puzzles over what an organisation is, and the fact that in many cases one organisation is actually wholly owned by another, it may be unclear for whom I am working. In effect I cannot make a free choice to work for firm *x* if I do not realise that the company that employs me is owned by firm *x*. This phenomenon is called *referential opacity*, and in this kind of case may be illustrated in Box 2.1:

BOX 2.1

REFERENTIAL OPACITY

I choose to work for company *z*

Company *z* is a wholly owned subsidiary of firm *x*

But I did not know this, and I did NOT choose to work for firm *x*

This contrasts with *referential transparency*, illustrated in Box 2.2

BOX 2.2

REFERENTIAL TRANSPARENCY

My work benefits company *z*

Company *z* is wholly owned by firm *x*

Therefore although I do not know this, my work benefits firm *x*

Overall, then, the transactional conception of work – that it is the performance of tasks in return for an anticipated reward – is not incoherent, though we have noted some shortcomings, particularly that it is less a material exchange and more a matter of intention, as well as (in some cases at least) the idea of reward and anticipation not necessarily being clear to the parties involved.

THE MEANING OF 'WORK'

2.2 It is one thing to establish the necessary and sufficient conditions to determine that some particular activity is, or is not, work. However, what is it like to *experience* work? What does this experience mean for the individual? When we turn to this question, it is important to recognise that the discussion of this particular book is taking place within a very specific set of social arrangements, namely the environment of a market economy, and it takes place at a time when there are few alternative socio-economic models in practice: this has not historically been the case generally. 'Work' here has thus been construed in its primary form as indicating activity within a market economy – once called, more simply, capitalism – and much of the discussion has revolved around the difficulties of specifying this concept exactly. But when we look at what work means to the worker, then we need to step outside of this particular historical frame of reference and consider the idea of work in more general terms.

One way to think of the experience of work is to contrast it with what is *not* work – mainly what we would call in broad terms leisure time. Once we do this then the interpretation of 'work' as being 'work in a market economy' becomes more evident. Some work (i.e. activity carried out as part of someone's paid occupation) is experienced in many ways rather like leisure – indeed for some people, such as musicians, sportspeople or artists, it cannot be distinguished from what they would do as leisure. They are both lucky and unusual, but this very fact indicates that what we normally call 'work' in *this* society reflects existing social presumptions. Norman Jackson and Pippa Carter discuss the idea of valuing idleness[1] – not quite the same as what I am here calling leisure but closely related. They argue that modern life has over-valued work to the extent that overworking has become a serious social problem. In this they make a well-recognised point. Their source for solving this problem, however, is not so much to do with the nature of work but with its *volume*. Idleness, in their view, is the way to combat the over-valuation of work. This is in itself an interesting position, but Jackson and Carter concede the idea that work is best construed in market-based terms.[2] In doing so, they exemplify the general point that discussions of work versus leisure can easily be encased in societal assumptions, even when authors are working to transcend them.

A number of writers have identified the importance of work, and related types of human activity, as being part of the nature of human life, and thus in some way they aim to get past assumptions associated with the market

---

[1] N. Jackson and P. Carter, *Workers of the World – Relax!* In *Philosophy and Organisation*, ed. Campbell Jones and Rene ten Bos (Routledge, 2007), pp. 143 ff.

[2] To give them their due, this is a deliberate intention on their part, not an oversight.

economy. In her book *The Human Condition*,[3] Hannah Arendt developed a deep-rooted critique of the role of work in modern society, drawing strong comparisons and contrasts between the present era and earlier societies. She distinguished three different categories of human activity, each of which was part of what she called *vita activa*. This latter phrase is difficult to interpret exactly, but for our purposes a fair summary is the literal translation of an 'active life', in the sense of living in a community with other humans, and contrasted with the more private idea of a *contemplative* life. The latter might well presuppose the former, but in itself it refers to life considered individually, privately, in isolation. This is not to say that an isolate, such as a Robinson Crusoe-type figure, could not behave in some of the ways that can be described by Arendt's model, so much as that such an individual could not enter into all the different kinds of activities that Arendt identifies.

Arendt talks of three distinct types of activity – to which she gives the labels *labour, work* and *action*. As we shall see she is using the terms in a specialised manner, which does not exactly follow common usage – not that this is a problem but it needs to be noted. However, these are not purely stipulative definitions; Arendt does argue that her distinctions, especially between labour and work, have resonances in many languages.

Arendt's understanding of *labour* is perhaps best understood in terms of how it differs from what she calls work. She talks of 'the labour of our bodies and the work of our hands', as well as seeing labour as relating to the basic necessities of life itself. The purest form of labour she identifies is the slave required to fetch and carry for their master. Labour in Arendt's sense is not necessarily unskilled work, but appears to represent the lowest form of human activity, characterised as activity alone and not considered in relation to anything it might bring about or produce. At one point Arendt seems to suggest that labour, in her sense, was in the past the kind of activity that servants and slaves carried out, in order that their masters or owners could live a free life ready to be productive in one way or another. Labour is non-productive, in contrast to work. Arendt goes out of her way to explain her view that even an activity such as ploughing the land remains at the level of labour, because on its own ploughed land is not something that can be made and once made used until it wears out – it is something that has to be tilled over and over again if it is to play any role in production.

Work, on Arendt's view, was to be identified with production. She used the Latin phrase *homo faber* (which roughly meant a craftsman in Roman times) and emphasised the linkage between the *activity* of work and its *outcome*. Work 'fabricates the ... things whose sum total constitutes the human artifice'.[4] By 'the human artifice' is meant the overall totality of our modern life with its machinery, goods and services, that 'create' the world

---

[3]H. Arendt, *The Human Condition* (University of Chicago Press, 1958).

[4]Ibid., Ch. IV, section 18.

in which we live. Associated, therefore, with work are its products – mostly things. Work is what changes the natural world into the things that make our life what it is.

Whereas labour and work involve the individual carrying on activities in relation to nature, Arendt's final category, *action*, refers to people carrying on activities between each other. In other words, 'action' refers to the social world that humans create around them. Often Arendt talks not of action on its own but of 'action and speech', the latter being the most direct and clear manifestation of the way in which people live with each other. Action thus encompasses not only social life but also political life – the manner in which different humans exist together to resolve their varying needs and projects.

To evaluate this, we need to ask what questions is Hannah Arendt trying to answer with this threefold categorisation of human activity? One key issue is how the different categories relate to each other, for it is clear that all three types of activity co-exist, even in the modern era. And this might suggest that these are the only three kinds of activity that characterise the human condition. However Arendt explicitly indicates that there are other features of what it is to be human – she mentions thought and reason, and elsewhere talks of 'human-created conditions' of life – so we must take the three categories of labour, work and action, not as the complete range of possible human activities, but as the basic conditions of a human life as we know it.

Another key question that Hannah Arendt was trying to answer was how far has the modern human condition developed in relation to earlier times – especially the well-developed political times of the ancient Greeks and Romans – and is there anything specially good or bad about the modern age? Her answer to this is not easily expressed, but essentially she is critical of the rise of the importance of the *vita activa* in comparison with the *vita contemplativa*. Activity has become the dominant aspect of the modern condition, displacing the traditional priority of thought and reflection. Further, the emphasis on activity has, on Arendt's view, displaced the sense of value in the things that are produced, and has focused instead on the value of actions as processes. There is yet a further paradox in this, that sheer activity, such as labour, becomes the most important part of production, as machine technology replaced craft. So the lowest of the three forms of activity becomes the most important for the modern age. Arendt thus sees the key fault of the modern age that process has pushed aside thinking and reflection.

Now, how does this account help us with our question – what does work mean for the worker? One feature of Arendt's analysis is that she wants to differentiate not only between different kinds of behaviour, but also between its different impacts on individuals and on society, and what that implies for the individual involved in such activity. In doing so she broadens out the kinds of things that we might consider as legitimate 'work', construed as behaviour that contributes to the life and well-being of individuals or society as a whole. Indeed, beyond the three aspects of the *vita activa* that she identifies, one would add the activity of reflection as being a further part of the range of behaviour that contributes to society, though Arendt herself would have argued that this has been excluded from modern conceptions of work.

On Arendt's view, work seems to have evolved from basic actions, through greater craft, through more socially oriented activity such as politics, to come round to a depleted emphasis in the modern age on basic activity, again in the form of mechanised and routinised acts, conforming to narrow specifications. Granted, she was writing over half a century ago. As a result there might appear to be a weakness in this argument, in terms of the growth of the idea of knowledge management, which clearly involves thought rather than 'basic' actions. However, her argument was not so much about the growth of completely mindless robotic activity as the loss of a sense of reflection as part of work. The modern knowledge worker is still arguably carrying out unreflective labour – simply the labour of the mind nowadays as opposed to that of the hands. One can see the rapid transactions of a money market broker as parallel to the labourer, in that improving the quality of work is absent from their perspective – improvement is not conceived in terms of 'better' contracts, but in simple increases in volume (in this case the volumes being of capital) and higher rates of return.

This discussion leads us to an important but perhaps over-used term in connection with working life – the idea that modern workers are *alienated* from their work. In other words the idea that a worker is separated from the results of their work – they do not choose exactly what work is to be done, they do not determine the manner in which it is done, and they do not possess the results of the work. Whilst Hannah Arendt criticised Marx's interpretation of work, she was strongly influenced by his view that modern forms of work alienate people from what they do.

Whilst the idea of alienation clearly incorporates a substantial element of evaluation in it – the whole idea of separation carries with it the suggestion that individuals would naturally be more closely linked to their work – nevertheless it helps us get a clearer idea of what it is like to be a worker. And the view of Arendt, like that of Marx, is that activity in the modern market economy[5] is deficient in addressing the full range of their natures. For Arendt this deficiency is in part located in the absence of reflection and contemplation in work.

Arendt's is not the only classification of different forms of work. Superficially similar, though serving a quite different purpose, is Pence's categorisation of labour, workmanship and *calling*.[6] By this latter term is meant the idea that someone derives a sense of identification, and likely deep pleasure, from carrying out their work. Although Pence uses the examples of musicians and great thinkers, the idea conceivably would not necessarily

---

[5] Whether or not we follow her in calling this labour, or retain the more natural term 'work'.

[6] G. Pence, 'Towards a theory of work', *Philosophical Forum* 10 (2-4), 1978/9.

preclude even the supposedly lowly ploughman, in cases where they did this in the right spirit. And this marks a key difference between his categorisation and that of Hannah Arendt, for the latter is based on the relation of the activity to the society in which it operates, whilst Pence's is based more on the intentions and experiences of the individual.[7]

But in one way Pence does take the discussion further, in that his idea of some work being a *calling* seems to echo some of the ideas of the more humanistic organisational psychologists, who look at work in terms of how it might contribute to human needs such as fulfilment.[8] On Pence's view, some occupations seem to blur the difference between what we often think of as work and leisure. His examples of people working in occupations that are traditionally regarded as creative (such as music, design or the arts in general) support this, for often many such people say that they would do what they do anyway, even if they were not paid to do so – and indeed other performers such as sportspeople sometimes say the same. So on Pence's view, the difference between what is work and what is not becomes less important than what kind of experience someone has in carrying out work. But consider the unusual example given in Box 2.3, where there is an economically significant event, carried out by an individual, but it is not clear what work has been done, if any at all. Work can involve a range of elements: the physical activity of work, intellective actions, the role of control in activity, the role of personal fulfilment and creative input, the extent to which people are integrated with or alienated from their activity, and of course the basic concept in a market economy of people selling the use of their skills and energies. These issues are not well captured definitionally, as we saw earlier, in part showing the limitations of definition in such an area. We have also seen that ethical attitudes are difficult to separate out here from descriptive explanation – that whatever understanding we have of work, it cannot be ethically neutral.

BOX 2.3

YVES KLEIN AND 'KLEIN BLUE'

The French artist Yves Klein (1928–1962) developed a new colour that is generally known in the artistic and printing world as 'International Klein Blue'. In doing this, he not only gave his name to it but also actually patented

(Continued)

[7]Though, he emphasises, not exclusively so.

[8]For example, the well known theories of motivation of Fred Herzberg or Abraham Maslow.

(Continued)

the process by which the colour might be produced (it is a particularly luminescent dark blue that cannot be easily replicated using normal printing processes). In effect then Klein came to 'own' this colour.

Now, although this is something Klein did for himself, not for others or for an organisation, it would seem to be an example of some kind of work. But it resists categorisation. True there is some kind of activity or labour here – the activity that uses chemical processes that lead to the production of the blue pigment. Workmanship too, in terms of the craft he used to formulate just that particular colour. But the key issue here is his laying claim to something that we would think of as being part of the natural world: it is almost like patenting the feeling of being warm.

The act of possession is clearly economically relevant behaviour, but although it usually involves some kinds of activities as necessary triggers for it to take place, the phenomenon of taking ownership in a case of this kind cannot be seen as a transaction, nor as activity in itself. The abstract nature of the action suggests that it is work without any physical manifestation.

HUMAN NATURE

2.3 Underpinning the discussion of the nature of work are assumptions about *human nature*. By this phrase is meant, loosely, what we basically are, as human beings. However, there is a range of questions relating to this idea, such as: how far is human nature fixed, or is it changeable; is human nature a purely biological concept, or does it reflect social influences as well; and more fundamentally, is there a single set of features that are necessary and sufficient for being human? We shall not discuss these directly – each of them would merit a book in its own right. But the comments below need to be interpreted in the light of these questions.

The main reason for considering what link there may be between working and some conception of human nature, is that there are significant consequences from identifying something as being part of our natures. For one thing, if a personal characteristic – say ambition – is seen as part of human nature, then purely on grammatical grounds we could infer that it is natural to be ambitious. For another, if a quality such as being ambitious is seen as human nature then people cannot be ethically criticised for at least being tempted to act in an ambitious way. Further, there is the argument that if something is part of our nature then it informs what ethical rights we may have – not that we simply have a right to act according to our basic nature, but that some of the rights we have may arise from what is natural to us. Indeed an ethical theory such as Aristotle's, based on the idea of what makes someone flourish, is rooted in assumptions about human nature.

Is work a basic aspect of humanity? Associated with Hannah Arendt's ideas on work is the idea of the *homo faber* – the human being as a creator. Indeed this underpins the idea that the separation of the individual from what they create is a form of alienation. In itself this does not automatically imply that it is intrinsic to the nature of humans that they work and create things, but one might ally this to the idea that a person's identity is expressed through their achievements and creations, which does suggest a sense in which human nature carries a direct linkage to their material activity. Indeed, most people, when asked about themselves, will answer in such a manner – I am an engineer, I am a teacher, I am a mother.[9] We will also see this idea of self-expression through work in some ideas of Hegel discussed in the following chapter.

Personal identity is not human nature; on the contrary it is what differentiates us from others, even when we share a common human nature (assuming that there is such a thing). But it is defined in terms of human nature, in the sense that my identity is the particular configuration of the elements that make up my humanity. If, however, someone regards part of their personal identity as defined by their work, then that would seem to suggest that work is indeed a core part of what it is to be human.

However, the idea of one's work as a defining feature of one's identity as a human being conflicts with our perception of other people as ethically equal to us. If work is part of our nature, then variations in the work we do might seem to imply variations in the way we are human. If one person can point to a range of very substantial activities and achievements, whilst a second has mainly lived a humdrum and relatively less directly productive life, surely we do not say that one has a *greater* human nature than the other? We might say many things about the greater impact or success or activity of the first person, but does that make them *more of a human being*? In previous centuries, when social status was be based on beliefs such as the divine right of kings, then perhaps the idea of greater and lesser people might have had some support. But in the present era it is generally accepted that sometimes at least achievement is *accidental* – the luck of being born in the right circumstances, or being in the right place to take advantage of an opportunity. Even many successful 'self-made' people, for whom achievement has been won by means of sacrifice and hard work, would acknowledge that the line between their success and failure at times was very thin. So the idea that some people have a 'greater' nature than others is not really plausible. This issue will come back when we discuss leadership in the following chapter.

There are other objections to the claim that one's work is an expression of one's human nature. Although many of us live in similar ways and produce similar outputs, there are some people – such as some artists, designers or engineers – who make unique and original contributions. Indeed some others might also be

---

[9]The last of these is included since some, but not all, mothers do regard the raising of their children as their most life-defining activity and achievement.

unique by virtue of their behaviour, their ways of befriending others, or even, more darkly, their ill-will towards others. But such uniquenesses do not imply that those individuals are categorically different from other humans – they do not have a different basic human nature, but rather the core elements of their humanity are configured (or even disfigured) in unusual ways.

Perhaps we might avoid these counter-arguments by saying that human nature includes the *capacity for working*, but not necessarily the *outcomes* of exercising that capacity. Although we might *socially* accord more status to people regarded as, for example, high achievers, that need not imply that we see them as superior in nature to others. There is a practical implication to this – much modern management writing focuses on success and achievement as a core aim. Whilst this is reasonable enough, the emphasis on this tends to downgrade the lives, contribution and experience of those who are not 'highly effective' or 'winners'. One can go further and state that such emphases can often lead individuals who cannot point to socially accepted 'successes' to feel that they are failures – almost, in effect, that *they have not fulfilled part of their very nature*. Furthermore this also seems to indicate that only certain forms of working activity are relevant to human nature, namely those aspects that will contribute to recognised outcomes such as career success, or professional achievement. In contrast, the view that what is central to human nature is the activity – working – and not the outcome is compatible with a range of different kinds of activity and different degrees of outcome.

The idea that work is part of being human has led to the idea that we can have a *right* to work, that in some sense the opportunity to be active is something that we can expect society to provide for us.[10] The rationale for this is that if work is part of our natures then we should have the space to express it. As we will see in Part Three of this book, to call something (such as work) a right is a complex assertion. It carries the suggestion that someone would be justified in demanding the opportunity to work, and further, that they should have the opportunity to assert that right. This can seem reasonable in the concrete practicalities of modern life, where there is clearly much that can be done that is socially and economically valuable even in times of recession and high unemployment. However, in the abstract there is a potential drawback to this. Imagine a very highly developed society, where technology is able to deliver all the goods and services that human beings need. How can the right to work be fulfilled here? While such a society is unlikely ever to come about, the idea alone undermines the concept of work as a fundamental right. Perhaps it is a right while there exist human needs that remain unfulfilled by society, but then that is not completely fundamental, but depends on other conditions being met.

---

[10]This is not the idea that the state, or government, has a duty to provide jobs for citizens, but rather the broader idea that the opportunity to work (for others or for oneself) is one of the benefits that one can expect or hope for in living in society.

We began this chapter in a similar vein to Chapter 1 – looking for simple definitions, sets of necessary and sufficient conditions that would capture what it is for someone to do work. In doing this we were implicitly seeking clarity for what has been described here as a 'standard' model of economic transaction – that one party gives something to another party as a trade for something else of value. The later discussion of what this means in experiential terms has of necessity been highly selective, though it should give a sense of the range of views relating to these two aspects of the market economy. The arguments over significance have been mainly critical. However they have been presented as representing views here and as noted above are not complete refutations of the standard conception of work. Indeed in some cases there are criticisms of the alternatives just as there are of the orthodoxy.

In the next chapter, the last of this first section, we will again start with the attempt to define a key phenomenon, in this case that of leading. Again we will encounter a blurring between a sheer explanation of what the phenomenon *is at all*, and what it is to have *a good example* of it. However, unlike this chapter, where this seemed to be intrinsic to the discussion, it can be more directly dealt with in the next.

QUESTIONS FOR REFLECTION

1 Is accepting and acting on a bribe a form of work – carrying out a task for payment by the person who offers you the bribe? If so why, and if not why not? Is your view changed if someone accepts a bribe but does *not* act on it?

2 Some people work, not specifically by carrying out activities, but for their character, to fulfil a role. A religious leader is one kind of example of this, or perhaps a Chief Executive taken on primarily as a figurehead, for their reputation. Whilst their fulfilment of the role might be measurable in terms of items such as impact on public opinion, it is not clear that what they actually do would necessarily be relevant to this (though of course it might be). So what kind of work is this, that seems not to relate to what someone *does* but what they might *be*?

FURTHER READING

Schaff, K. (ed.) (2001) *Philosophy and the Problems of Work*. Rowman and Littlefield.
The discussion of work has a parallel in the concept of the consumer or customer. The following are contributions to that parallel debate about the nature of consumption in modern society.
Baudrillard, J. (1998) *The Consumer Society*. Sage (originally published in French in 1970).
Klein, N. (2001) *No Logo*. 4th Estate.
Schwartz, B. (2005) *The Paradox of Choice: why more is less*. HarperCollins.

LEADING IN ORGANISATIONS

After reading this chapter you should be able to:

- identify elements in the process of leading
- evaluate the asymmetry between leaders and followers.

So far the search for definitions has told us something about the concepts involved, but has not fully clarified the terms in question. One lesson to draw from this is that sometimes definitions cannot capture the full range of examples of a certain term. Therefore, although in this chapter we are aiming to understand what 'leader' means, we will not exhaustively search for a definition in the sense of a set of necessary and sufficient conditions.

EXPLORING THE MEANING OF 'LEADER'

3.1 Leadership is probably the most common notion in the theory of organisations. As a result the literature abounds with definitions, models, categorisations and other attempts to understand what they mean. There are two difficulties that arise from this abundance. Firstly, in some cases the language can become self-certifying. Anthony Giddens has talked about how some words become ingrained in public discourse, even though in fact they may represent contentious ideas.[1] He calls this phenomenon the *double hermeneutic*, meaning that specialist theoretical language becomes generally accepted, and thus integrated into the common stock of terms used. As a result many explanatory models and definitions become integrated into common discourse without their particular nuances or evidential support being fully appreciated.

---

[1]Anthony Giddens, *Social Theory and Modern Sociology* (Polity Press, 1987). The term 'double' hermeneutic is used, because the process Giddens describes is the inverse of, and addition to, the standard 'hermeneutic' process, whereby ordinary discourse gives rise to, and becomes absorbed by, specialised theoretical language.

An example of this is provided by ideas such as 'transformational' leadership,[2] or 'action-centred' leadership.[3] In both cases there is a positive nuance in the key terms – 'action' sounds like a model that gets on with things, so it becomes attractive for the busy manager; similarly, 'transformational' sounds far reaching, creating an impression that this will solve major problems. So the terminology, whether fully understood or not, finds its way into common discourse, and in doing so drifts away from its original meaning. This is not to say that ideas are valuable or not, nor is it anything to do with the intentions of the writers. The point here is simply that models and their associated terminology can become absorbed into common parlance without them being properly understood, and thus people may then construe an idea such as leadership as meaning *exactly what that particular model denotes*. So we have the trend where a whole community of users of a range of terms drawn from theoretical models may regard these as *equivalent in meaning* to the more day-to-day terms they purport to explain.

The second issue that complicates discussions about management or leadership is that most discussion is aimed at identifying what can help someone to become *good* at these. In focusing on leader*ship* (as opposed to just leading) such discussions aim to understand the *craft* of being a leader. Indeed some of the models openly use terminology that is explicitly evaluative. For example the well-known 'managerial grid' of Blake and Mouton[4] talks of 'middle of the road' management, and 'impoverished' management – terms that clearly suggest whether or not they are desirable.

The focus on terminology in this discussion raises the question: is there such a phenomenon as 'leadership', or have we have been beguiled by the existence of words into believing that they reflect something in reality? Once one looks beyond English, other languages use a range of terms that refer in different ways to those people who are responsible for organisations, as well as often importing derivatives of the English word 'leadership'. 'Leader' derives from old English and Norse words based on the idea of going or travelling. Italian, French and Spanish all use a term deriving from the idea of *direction*, which comes from Latin roots based on the idea of ruling or guiding. Other languages have yet other terms.[5]. Hence, given that we have a range of terms of varying origins, perhaps none of them fully

---

[2]See J. Burns, *Leadership* (Harper and Row, 1978).

[3]See J. Adair, *Effective Leadership* (Pan, 1988).

[4]R. Blake and J.Mouton, *The Managerial Grid: The Key to Leadership Excellence* (Gulf Publishing, 1964).

[5]Languages as diverse as Filipino and Turkish not only use words that are structural variants of the English term leadership but also have local terminology that has evolved independently. As with the reference to Italian, French and Spanish terms given in the text, many other languages appear to rely frequently on terms more closely linked with the idea of *direction* than leadership.

captures the whole of 'leadership'. So it is arguable that this variability of terms indicates that what we have here is not a well founded concept at all.

Having said this, we will adopt the working hypothesis that there is a unified phenomenon that can be called leadership, if only to see what problems may arise from this. Whilst the main focus of the discussion is on leaders and leadership, some points will also be applicable to the idea of a manager. But the main intention is to understand *what it is* to lead: not how to be a good leader, but to be a leader at all.

In what follows we shall look at a cluster of ideas relating to the three key elements of leadership – namely, the leader, the followers, and the kind of influence that leaders may have over their followers.

CONDITIONS FOR LEADING

3.2 We will start by looking at what circumstances need to be present for leadership to happen at all. When can someone lead, and when is it not possible? Clearly a leader has to lead someone. And the followers must stand in some kind of relationship to the leader: they have some direct communication with the leader, and at least some of their actions are in line with the wishes of the leader. A group of people who simply happen always to do what someone else wants them to do are not followers. They must be doing something specifically *in virtue* of the wishes of someone if that person is to be regarded as their leader.

Leadership is clearly linked closely with getting people to follow – influencing, in fact. Indeed, some management textbooks explicitly put the two concepts together.[6] But is leadership exactly the same as getting people to do things? Gangsters can be leaders, and exert influence over other gang members (who therefore could be described as followers) not only by the usual methods of exhortation and reward but also by high levels of coercive and threatening behaviour. But what about those whom the gangster exploits, their victims – for example a shopkeeper forced to pay protection money? They may be influenced to do what the gangster wants, but they are not *following* the gangster in the way that the other mobsters do, rather they are *complying* with what the gangster wants. Is the difference one of willingness – that the follower willingly goes along with the leader, whilst the victim is forced against their will? But that might not exclude gang members, who may be threatened with violence if they choose no longer to follow the gangster. So leading and following are more than simply getting someone else to do something.

A more plausible account of the difference between leading and merely influencing, might be to say that the acts of leading and following *create*

[6]For example David Boddy's *Management* (FT Prentice Hall, 4th edition, 2008) does not have a separate chapter in leadership, but incorporates his main discussion of that concept in his chapter on power and influence.

a particular kind of social group. The leader and the followers are united, willingly or not, by their actions. The unwilling victim is not linked in the same way as part of a social arrangement, even if the gangster continues their exploitation of the victim over an extended period. A victim is 'outside' the social arrangement, whilst a follower (whether they like it or not) is 'inside'. Being identified as following someone else can imply that one is identified with their views and beliefs. This is not only true of great ideological leaders such as politicians and religious gurus, but also of companies, where members of a certain team might be identified with or even blamed for the views of their leader – even when they do not actually share those views. The presumption is that a person who follows someone else is *connected* with the leader – perhaps indicating that they share the beliefs of the leader, or have some special understanding of the leader's thoughts.

But this explanation raises further questions. Whilst a group of individuals with a leader is not necessarily the same thing as an organisation, it may encounter some of the identification issues we saw in Chapter 1 – how do we recognise such notional things as social groups? Where are their boundaries? When is someone 'in' and someone 'out' of such a social entity? There are probably no simple boundaries to such groups, but they exist on a continuum – at one end someone is a member of a group and at the other end they are not, though no clear point of transition is evident.

The preceding paragraphs imply that communication must take place between leader and followers, if any leading at all is to happen. Not that communication is necessarily conscious, or verbal – some successful leaders can get people to do things without explicitly stating it at all. But if a group of people simply decided to do something without any idea at all of whether their supposed leader wanted this or not, then we would probably describe this as the followers being out of the leader's control.

Communication may take place at different levels with contrasting implications, and sometimes may be badly done, confused, or simply misunderstood. Thus a leader may be responsible for acts of their followers that they never intended. This supports the suggestion made earlier, that the leader–follower relationship in part creates a certain kind of social grouping, one which involves the identification of members with the views and acts of their leader, and vice versa.

A further aspect of the conditions of leading is how far being a leader implies anything about time or space. Can you be a leader for a few hours? Probably. For a few minutes? Perhaps in certain circumstances, such as a major emergency. But there must be some lower limit beneath which one would say that someone was no longer leading others but just happened to get them to do something. So leading people seems to imply some degree of persistence or duration.

In terms of space, does being a leader imply anything about contact or closeness with followers? Metaphorically one might say that there needs to be some kind of 'space' that both leader and followers occupy, in order for any kind of communication to pass between them. By 'space' here is meant the existence of some kind of environment within which communications can take place. These might be electronic, physical, written communications or by proxy – before the telephone age the influence that a leader had over followers operating in remote areas was almost always expressed by personal representatives travelling to those areas.

One final point worth noting at this stage is that leading and following do not directly imply a conscious awareness of the relationship – it would be possible for someone to have followers without ever realising this, and equally for people to follow someone and not recognise that they are doing so. Indeed, theories of 'informal' organisation, where organisational structures do not capture exactly the power relationships between members of the organisation, may exemplify this phenomenon in some cases.

So far we have established that: (a) leading appears to create a social entity that includes the leader and followers but excludes others, even when their actions might be influenced by the leader, and (b) there are minimal parameters for the leadership role in terms of time, but more significantly in terms of space, at least in the sense of a 'space' for contact and communication to take place between leader and followers.

HOW MUCH DO LEADERS INFLUENCE EVENTS?

3.3 In the case of great leaders of the past there are continuing controversies over how far they *made* things happen, as opposed to merely being the symbols of events that would have happened somehow anyway. Leo Tolstoy, the Russian writer, was firmly of the camp that diminishes the role of the individual leader. In his novel *War and Peace* he describes Napoleon at the head of a great army, and asks whether he could have simply stopped and told the half million or so soldiers behind him, marching (in their view) to victory, to turn around and head home. Tolstoy's view is that the impetus of events made such a move impossible. One might object that at *some* points the impetus of events might have been too great for a leader to turn the tide, but this does not imply that there are *no points at all* when a leader can change the course of events: for example one might say that Napoleon could have avoided starting a war in the first place.

The opposite extreme to this is the so-called 'great man'[7] view of history – that events are indeed determined by the decisions and intentions of the most vigorous and capable individuals involved – who are generally identified as

---

[7] I intentionally use this term despite the gender specificity, for two reasons: one is that this has been the phrase generally used for this theory, and two, in most discussions, the leaders referred to have been male – kings, generals, dictators etc.

leaders. Although this view has been regularly criticised, it remains a popular line of thought in many books on leadership.[8] Both Plato and Machiavelli, well represented in discussions of leadership, regarded the leader (prince, king, guardian etc.) as someone uniquely qualified to hold and exercise power due to specific aspects of their personality.[9] What is often held to follow from this is that the individuals in question are above ordinary morality. There are hints of this kind of individualism in several discussions of political leadership, such as Machiavelli's idea that the Prince has a certain kind of personal quality that gives him the right to act autonomously from 'ordinary' mores.[10] Indeed this represents one form of the conception of a social *elite*.

It hardly needs saying that human beings vary in their levels of knowledge, skill and understanding, as well as in their long-term plans and projects, and even the way in which their basic needs and wants are expressed. In general these differences are not in themselves accepted as a basis for exempting people from standards of behaviour. We might, it is true, exempt some individuals if it is felt that they cannot help themselves – say if they have substantial learning deficits. But the idea that someone can be *too smart* to be subject to ethical or other social norms does not follow from this.

It would take us too far from our current discussion to debate the merits and demerits of the concept of elitism. Whilst the present era favours more egalitarian principles than much of history, the idea of an elite has had its supporters over many centuries, for example it is a central idea in the political writings of both Plato and Confucius.[11] The main thing for us to note here is that it underpins concepts such as the well-known trait theory of leadership, the idea that some people have certain features of their personality – character traits – that fit them to be leaders, in contrast to those who may lack these traits.

---

[8]See for example Jonathan Gifford's *History Lessons: What Business and Management can Learn from the Great Leaders of History* (Marshall Cavendish, 2010). To be fair on Gifford, his book is less a celebration of the 'great man' thesis than an attempt to illustrate the idea of good leadership from historical figures. Nevertheless, it arguably reflects the idea that these individuals had a determining influence over the events in which they were involved.

[9]An example of the extreme individualism that this implies may be found in the work of the German Philosopher Friedrich Nietzsche, who talked of the 'superman' and of the individual who is above ordinary ethics (which he called 'slave-morality') possessing instead a 'will to power'. Nietzsche's conception thus seems to divide people into those who rise above ordinary social norms and values, and those who are more suited to acceptance of those norms.

[10]His term for these qualities was '*vertu*' but it was not intended in the same sense as our modern usage of the word 'virtue', referring instead to a kind of insightful daring. Cf. *The Prince* chs 6 and 7.

[11]See *The Analects of Confucius*, trans. C. Huang (OUP, 1997) e.g. books 2 and 8.

BOX 3.1

KAGEMUSHA

The feature film *Kagemusha* ('shadow warrior' or impersonator in Japanese), written and directed by Akiro Kurosawa, depicts a low-status criminal who is first asked to act as a double for a great warlord, but when the warlord dies he is required to continue permanently as that warlord. In time the criminal 'learns' to act as the warlord and fools all around him apart from the officials who originally set the doubling up. But after a battle it is discovered that he is not the warlord, and he is cast out. Part of the tragedy is that he retains his new-found commitment to his role, and enters the final battle dying even as his status has returned to that of being just a thief.

As a leader, the kagemusha starts with only a physical resemblance, but eventually acquires the skills of diplomacy and warfare, discharging his duties effectively and with honour. But he is eventually rejected not because he is not fit to lead – he has proved that he is – but because *he is not a particular person*. It is the specific identity as a certain individual that was required of this leadership role, not their skills or knowledge. Being a leader, then, sometimes is a little like a painting: however good the resemblance, a substitute is not the 'real' thing.

This difference of focus – between the individual who acts as a figurehead for events over which they may have little if any control, and the individual who controls, directs, and even creates events – underlines a key element in understanding what a leader is. The idea of influence that underpins being a leader is that the desires of the leader *explain* the behaviour of the followers. This indicates why followership is not merely doing something that someone else (i.e. the leader) wishes. It is doing something *because* the leader wishes it. We will turn now to the idea of a follower.

FOLLOWERS

3.4 As well as the leader's influence over followers, in some way those followers must have some impact on the leader. Leaders are often held responsible for the acts of their followers, even when they do not approve of them, so to that degree at least the acts of followers affect a leader. What kind of communication might pass from followers to leader, which might have an influence on their actions? One aspect is that someone leading a group of people needs to have some feedback from them, if only to know that those other people are in fact following at all. Even where there is direct coercion, influencing others involves not simply persuading or inspiring but also *gauging the feelings* of others, since there is always the possibility that the followers might refuse to follow. A degree of two-way communication is therefore implied by this. And this is not a point about being a *good* leader, but being a leader at all. If someone is to lead in *any* sense then they have to have an idea of the capacity of others to follow, at the lowest level even who is there to follow, and on what basis they might be prepared to follow.

To properly understand what it is to be a follower it is worth considering the various reasons why someone might choose to follow someone else. In some cases there may be direct benefits from doing so – sometimes the leader is the cleverest, most effective individual in the group, and allowing them to lead will provide the best opportunity of achieving the outcomes the followers wish for. In other cases, the social structure has already designated someone as a leader, and any attempts to overcome this will be self-defeating, as when one member of a work team is of a higher grade than others.

Maccoby[12] has argued that following can be seen as a form of Freudian *transference* – the individual follows someone because they project on to them feelings transferred from their mother and/or father – the leader is thus a psychological replacement for the parent. Maccoby also suggests that the leader may counter-transfer, treating their followers as a psychological replacement for children. But it is not at all clear that Freudian analysis always applies; consider a ten-year-old boy leading a group of seven-year-olds in a team game. Would we say that these children are engaged in this form of transference? Whilst it is not impossible, the whole idea seems more suited to adult relationships than child-to-child ones. But the ten-year-old is still *leading*, and the seven-year-olds are still *following*, even if the context is relatively unusual.

A more raw, primitive idea is that when one person follows another they are *subjected to that person's will*. The German philosopher Georg Hegel suggested that what he called the Master–Slave relationship is a fundamental feature of human relationships. Hegel's argument is very abstract, and has been interpreted in widely differing ways. But to elucidate his key idea, Hegel provides an account that is highly poetical in nature, almost a myth.[13]

Imagine a conscious individual, in isolation, living freely and without depending on anyone else, in fact not recognising that anyone else like them exists. Then along comes another individual who equally exists without a dependence on or recognition of anyone else. The encounter

---

[12]M. Maccoby, *The Leaders We Need* (Harvard Business School Press, 2007).

[13]G.W.F. Hegel, *Phenomenology of Spirit*, trans. A.V. Miller (Clarendon Press, 1977; original publication 1807).

of the two individuals makes them self-conscious – aware not just of themselves but also that at least one other being exists like them. When these two individuals confront each other – and here is Hegel's first major claim – each attempts to continue to exert power over their environment, which now means *trying to make the other person obey their will.* Hegel depicts this as a struggle, which he calls, fancifully, a fight to the death. However, this struggle rarely ends in death. The fear of death leads one or other person to yield. In yielding they become the slave, and the 'victor' becomes the master.[14] But here is a second implication of Hegel's argument: it is the *slave* who has developed the deeper consciousness. It is the 'loser' who embraces not only the reality of their own thoughts and intentions, but also those of their master. The master, on the other hand, continues as if there is no other reality than their own conception, because they have exerted the power to prevent any other reality from being expressed, in effect.

However, this is not a stable situation – the slave gradually recognises their own identity through their work, whilst the master becomes dependent on the slave's production. And this is a third key point of the analogy – the 'winner' in such a struggle is not thereby better off. Their 'victory' brings them, not only a limitation on their consciousness, but also a level of material dependence on those whom they are supposed to have mastered. We might say, in the context of leadership, that Hegel's argument suggests that leaders are often less developed individuals than those they lead.

This myth has been variously used and developed to explain a range of political views, notably revolutionary or reforming movements such as Marxism, feminism and anti-colonialism. It is important to recognise that it is intended as an analogy, not as a depiction of reality. For the present discussion, it is best considered as a thought experiment to focus attention on the nature of the asymmetry between leader and followers.[15]

There are resonances here with the ideas of Chris Argyris, who has coined the phrase *'the undiscussability of the undiscussable'*[16] by which he means that senior managers in organisations sometimes do not simply impose their views on the firm, do not even refuse to discuss this, but *refuse even to consider that there is an issue* to be discussed. In Hegelian language we might see this as the master imposing their conception of events on their slave(s),

---

[14]And indeed the slave continues to live under the fear that the master will fight to the death if their authority is challenged.

[15]It is probably worth adding here that Hegel's aim in presenting this myth is as much about understanding what self-consciousness is and how we achieve recognition, as in depicting the relationship between the self and others.

[16]C. Argyris, *On Organisational Learning*, 2nd edn (Blackwell, 1999) ch. 4.

by refusing to give room for debate. One of Argyris' points is that at times many managers – despite believing themselves to be highly consultative and facilitative – fall into the trap of inhibiting discussion in exactly the way outlined. One can put this too in a Hegelian context: the Master may coerce others to accept their perception of events, but in doing so they blinker themselves to an alternative reading of reality, and they may convince themselves that the Slave has not been forced to accept their view, but has instead come round to it of their own accord.

The myth of the master–slave relationship presents a paradoxical view of leaders. Generally in discussions of leadership, attention is focused on the leader as possessing something extra, as we saw earlier – greater power, competence, or simply the support of others. But here we see one way in which the *follower* has something extra – the understanding of both their own and the master's points of view, as well as the expression of their identity through work.

Hegel's view of such interpersonal relationships is not compatible with much modern leadership literature, where ideas such as inspiration, authenticity and consultation all present the leader as reaching out to their followers, suggesting that the follower needs to be *wooed* rather than struggled with. There is a direct connection between Hegel's view of the master–slave relationship as one of struggle and fear, and Machiavelli's notorious concept of the Prince as being a person who rules by the exercise of power, this in turn being more effectively done by means of fear than by appeals to authority, legality or affection.

So which is the better guide as to the nature of leading – the modern, consultative, involvement-based models, or the more conflict oriented, coercive conception? Although almost every contemporary account of leadership would probably reject the coercive conception of Hegel, in reality the question is misplaced. Most current models of leadership are essentially dealing with the question of *what is good leadership*, whereas our discussion is explicitly about what is leadership *per se*. The Hegelian master–slave myth depicts leadership in extreme terms, but it highlights an element in all leader-to-follower relationships. For whilst the idea of a struggle to the death is rather far-fetched, nevertheless the power differential between leader and followers – particularly in organisations – is generally based on the possibility of sanction.

For example, consider organisational conflict between managers. Differences in ideas of policy direction often mask the competition for advancement, control of key resources, or increase in power. Such differences are manifest in events such as boardroom disputes or presentations of competing strategic plans. The conflict gets resolved with one or other party being perceived as having had the better of an argument. And in the extreme, where the parties maintain their dispute beyond normal decision-making processes, there is the possibility of dismissal – the organisational analogue of death. So the Hegelian 'struggle to the death' may well have an echo in the ability and willingness of one party to invoke organisational processes to exert their will, even to the point of risking dismissal. It would oversimplify to say that the modern organisation has the power to force its members to submit to the will of its leadership, but the fact that companies in advanced economies have remained hierarchical rather than progress to full democracy underlines the role of dominance and submission in organisational experience.

But does the other side of Hegel's argument work? Do followers in organisations have some kind of deeper understanding than leaders? Though this looks factually false, one can construct an interpretation that points to something not normally seen in leadership discussions. The point about Hegel's myth is that the slave not only has their own consciousness, but is also forced to accept the consciousness of the master as well. Continuing the link with Argyris's idea of undiscussability, it can be claimed that the leader by refusing to countenance debate about an issue protects their own perception, whilst the followers do not stop having their own perception of the situation; they just are not allowed to express it. The leader – i.e. the 'Master' – retains a single, unchallenged, conception of the firm, whilst the employees – the 'Slaves' – are obliged to retain two different conceptions: their own, unexpressed, ideas, and the officially authorised conception that the Master holds. The analogy is not exact however. Hegel goes on to argue that the slave finds some degree of authenticity in the experience of producing goods for their master, whereas the employee in a modern firm does not necessarily have that option, and even when they do have a degree of autonomy in the details of their work, the underlying design of an organisational value chain still imposes a non-negotiable element on the ultimate form and ends of what an employee can do.

To summarise this section, the Hegelian master–slave myth can be used to depict leadership as a defective condition, arising from a deep-rooted need to maintain dominance over others. However, whilst this may reflect much organisational experience, it is not a complete account of the leader–follower relationship.

LEADERSHIP AND EQUALITY

3.5 The Hegelian conception outlined above is contentious, carrying with it the implication that leadership is inherently a defect in a human character. Of the many alternative accounts of leading and following that may be outlined, one that is based on the views of Hegel's great predecessor, Immanuel Kant, is noteworthy. Norman Bowie outlines a Kantian view of what it is to lead, based on the idea of autonomy, a central element of

Kant's ethical theory.[17] Bowie specifically rejects the vision of leadership as dominance, and looks at it as a rational interaction between equals.

Bowie first of all criticises an approach to leadership that is almost the direct opposite of the Hegelian 'mastery' conception – an idea that Bowie calls *servant leadership* – the idea that the best leaders are those who present themselves as 'servants' to the team and the task they are promoting, on the grounds that they are therefore most likely to be successful. His argument here is that despite its apparent humility, this move still depicts one individual as placed at the disposal of another, treated no longer as human in their own right but only in so far as they contribute to the other's ends. Bowie bases this on Kant's ethical view that all rational beings are to be treated equally. Kant's argument is that a rational being is one who founds their actions on reason rather than on inclinations or desires. So if one human being sees a reason for doing something, then this must be so for others as well. Bowie argues that this egalitarian view is inconsistent with the idea of super- and subordination implicit in the servant theory of leadership. Presumably he would also deploy the same kind of argument against the Hegelian view outlined earlier. But Bowie's use of this argument to support modern, egalitarian, approaches such as *transformational leadership*, may itself be criticised.

The Kantian conception requires all rational beings to treat each other, and each other's decisions, as meriting equal consideration. This does not necessarily mean that we have to agree with everyone else's choices, but rather that we regard them as just as well founded as our own. Arguably, though, one does not try to transform other people's ideas unless in some way one thinks that they are *wrong*. Now, on its own this does not undermine the idea of equality between individuals. But Kant's view of this equality is specifically related to his idea of ethics as being based on reason. His argument relates to the equality of individuals as rational agents, who act from essentially the same basic motive – to act in line with what one thinks is one's duty.

'Transformation' is more than merely change. It suggests a far-reaching realignment of someone's ideas, their values, their basic conceptions. But on a Kantian view rational beings *already share* the same fundamental value. Whilst change is possible, perhaps by bringing forward facts that someone else did not know, the *transformation* of one person's view by another indicates that the first person has a more limited understanding than the second. Transformations can and do happen – it is what the learning process in all of our lives involves. But they represent a *growth* in rationality. Kant's view does not contradict this but neither does it explain it. Hence it is misleading for Bowie to regard models such as transformational leadership as being egalitarian in Kant's sense of the term.

---

[17]N. Bowie (2000) 'A Kantian theory of leadership', *Leadership & Organization Development Journal*, 21 (4): 185–93.

The most important point that we can draw from this discussion is the *asymmetry* between leader and followers. In some way, a leader's ideas and intentions of what should happen are given priority over the views of others. Even models of leadership that talk about transformation or authenticity still assume that the leader is in a special position, in that their choices take precedence over those of followers. This does not lead to the (false) consequence that a leader's ideas are the only ones that are accepted or implemented. But it does indicate that the leader's ideas take greater priority, and where an individual challenges the leader's views, it is the prerogative of the leader to decide whether to consider or reject that challenge.

The key lessons that we draw from this discussion of followers are (a) leaders are in part identified with the actions of their followers; (b) whilst leaders have an influence on the acts of their followers, followers have an influence, albeit less direct, on leaders; (c) in view of the fact that the follower not only has their own thoughts and intentions, but also accepts the thoughts and intentions of their leader, they may have a broader perception than the leader, who needs only to be clear as to their own intentions; (d) there is an asymmetry between leader and follower, based on power, which is particularly evident in terms of the choices the leader makes.

One interesting implication of these points relates back to the idea of leaders as 'great men', and somehow different from others. This was construed in the context of that difference being a superiority of the leader over their followers. But in this discussion the difference is in effect an *inferiority*. Doubtless this was not what writers such as Machiavelli had in mind. We need, though, to note that such a deficit need not be permanent; once someone ceases to occupy the dominant role then the circumstances in which the asymmetry existed disappear.

In conclusion, consider the question raised towards the start of this chapter. How far is 'leader' a clear concept, or is this a case where the use of a word deceives us into thinking, incorrectly, that there is a unified idea behind it? We have not seen enough to give a definitive response to this. The range of models and theories used to provide explanations of leadership – masters and slaves, Freudian transference, 'great men' and so on – suggests at least that a single underlying idea of what a leader is has not been fully captured. We will leave this discussion with a suggestion that perhaps here is a good example of what Wittgenstein called family resemblance: maybe 'leader' is not completely explained by any single statement of meaning that covers all cases, but represents a cluster of different cases, that have loose similarities in various ways, without fitting a single formula.

QUESTIONS FOR REFLECTION

1   There is a well known saying 'A man cannot serve two masters'. This idea is often breached in modern organisations, especially those adopting matrix structures. How is this possible, and can there ever be complete equality in multiple leadership situations?

2   Does following necessarily require someone to believe in the same ideas as the leader? How would you describe a situation where one person followed another solely on the basis of having calculated that there was a specific benefit (e.g. professional advancement) they could obtain by doing so?

FURTHER READING

Aristotle, *Politics*, Book V (Of Revolutions) (Penguin Classics, 2000).
Confucius, *The Analects*, trans. C. Huang (Oxford University Press, 1997).
Kellerman, B. *Followership,* (Harvard Business School Press, 2008).

CONCLUSION
OF PART ONE

In this first section of the book, we have looked at a range of key concepts –
leading, working, organisation – with a view to clarifying their meaning
and in some cases also their existence. In all three cases we saw that there is
a degree of *intention* that enters into the understanding of these ideas.
Whilst we feel confident about which bodies are standard examples of
organisations, and of non-organisations, there are problematic cases such as
one- or two-person partnerships that are not easy to describe completely in
that manner. We have seen also that working relationships cannot be fully
explained on an exchange or transactional model, even if this provides
some of our understanding of these concepts. And we have seen that the
idea of leading often, erroneously, involves an idea of the superiority of the
leader over their followers, when it could be argued that in some ways a
leader lacks something that the followers have.

Some issues have recurred, not quite so systematically that we would call
them themes, but often enough to merit their being emphasised. One is the
shortcoming of definition. In the main our search for definitions has been
inconclusive. This is not to imply that the ideas dealt with are all meaningless. But it does indicate that the search for clarity and understanding of key
concepts, in management as in other fields, is often more complex and can
involve more issues that is commonly supposed. The seventeenth-century
English philosopher Thomas Hobbes once said, as a criticism, 'People often
think that when they have words in their mouths, they have ideas in their
minds.' Such a note of caution needs to be carried forward to the next part
of this book, where we will look at knowledge and thought in management.

A second recurring issue is the tendency for questions that look to be simply categorical to point towards ethical considerations. In neither the discussions of work nor of leading was this tendency unmanageable, but it raises
the question of whether *any* questions in a practice oriented field such as
management can be completely divorced from questions about what should
be done. Arguably our attempt to discuss leadership, in particular, in isolation from the idea of what is good leadership may have missed the point.
However, it is important to attempt such a task even if it is not successful.

A third issue is the political context. As the dominant ideology governing business and organisations is favourable to the market economy, several points of critique in these chapters have been directed, beyond specific

issues such as working or consumption, to the overall corporate environment within which these practices currently exist. This should not be taken as evidence that a philosophical account of management must necessarily be anti-capitalist, any more than that it should support the status quo. The key aim of any philosophical discussion is to uncover assumptions and where possible clarify the justification of given positions regarding the deepest questions of existence, right and knowledge. Where discussion identifies unchallenged assumptions it is almost a duty to at least consider what challenges may be made to these, as a matter of course.

In Section 2 we will look at the issue of knowledge as it relates to organisations. We will find that the 'what?' questions we have considered here will recur, both as part of the context of the discussion, but also as objects of the discussion in the sense that what we say about knowledge in organisations may refine further some of our ideas about what an organisation is and the various roles people may take in relation to them.

THINKING AND KNOWING ABOUT MANAGEMENT

2

In Section 1 we looked at definitions of some key concepts of management –
above all the organisation, the leader, and work. One thing we saw is that
when trying to focus specifically on what something is (as opposed to, say,
what it ought to be) it was difficult in most cases to find a single form of
words that captured all the cases we would normally and instinctively think
of as examples of the idea in question. As Chapters 2 and more especially 3
progressed, we focused ever more on what it might *mean* to apply the concept in question. This became most evident when we discussed ideas about
what it is to be a leader, where we found that the sense, or the experience, of
leading is quite removed from traditional discussions of leadership – that is, of
what makes someone a good leader.

Another area that could be questioned is what exactly do we *know* about
management? We presume that knowledge about management should be
the kind of thing that tells us something general about managers or organisations – or at least a defined category of these. Perhaps something of the
form that states that in certain defined situations, technique x is most effective, or perhaps even that most managers would do a rather than b. But is
this true in all cases? If not, then is it *knowledge*, or just a good approximation? Consider that even one human being is immensely complex, with a
whole history of years of experience, with many thoughts and perceptions
that they may not always give full expression to (and so others do not know
they are there) and with a cluster of needs and driving forces that even they
do not fully understand – and now multiply that by the number in even a
small firm, with all the interactions and communication networks, and it
becomes amazing that we get anything right about such collections of people.
Once one adds in the vast complexity of markets, then the idea of solid
knowledge that applies across a whole category of organisations or their
operations looks extremely optimistic.

Maybe we are looking for the wrong thing. Maybe we should try to find
out what managers themselves know about the job. Talk to any practising manager and they will probably rely on the lessons they have learnt

from their personal experience, but these are usually particular to them, and often not expressed very precisely – 'always cover your back' is one example of this kind of experience-based 'knowledge' but it is not likely that this applies in all cases: sometimes it is necessary to take risks, leaving your 'back' exposed. So this bit of advice is more like a rule of thumb than a piece of knowledge that we can rely on in all cases.

But are we asking too much? Maybe what we call knowledge in relation to management is not the same kind of thing that we would expect from, say, natural science or a court of law, where we would like to establish something beyond reasonable doubt. But then what is knowledge when we apply it to organisations and their management? Maybe the answer is that for management we use a different sense of the word.

In Section 2 we will explore these questions of knowledge more fully. The field we are looking at is known as *epistemology* – the philosophical study of knowledge. We will apply the lessons of this field to knowledge and thought as they relate to organisations and management. In doing so, we will find at times that the discussion refers us back to issues about what the key concepts really are, and how do things covered by these concepts exist – the definitional questions of Section 1 – but also we will find that the discussion flags forward in places to issues of what is right or wrong in management. Knowledge is of what there is, but it informs what we do – so this section, as well as having its own value in itself, also functions as a bridge between the ontological discussions of Section 1 and the ethical ones which we will encounter in Section 3.

Structurally this section of the book first of all discusses some of the key *questions* relating to knowledge as these apply to management, then it looks at some of the standard *answers* to these questions, following which we will look at the extent to which knowledge is culturally determined, and how far we can learn from philosophies from outside the main European traditions. This part of the book will then end with a discussion of the concept of knowledge management, a concept which in some formulations explicitly draws on philosophical ideas about knowledge.

QUESTIONING OUR KNOWLEDGE ABOUT MANAGEMENT

4

After reading this chapter you should be able to:

- critically identify arguments concerning our knowledge of the external world, in relation to the context of business
- evaluate definitions of knowledge in terms of belief and justification
- evaluate the ideas of a foundation for knowledge, and of knowledge as coherence.

KNOWLEDGE IN BUSINESS

4.1 Our every action is informed by knowledge or beliefs about the world around us. Most of the time we act without questioning these, but when we do question them, often we do not have sufficient evidence to justify them. There are two aspects to this, that distinguish two different sides to philosophical discussions about knowledge. First we can question whether *in specific cases* we have sufficient evidence to justify our claim that we know, say, that the global economy is in recession. We might call these questions about what things we know and why. In contrast, the other kind of questions would be about what we think *our knowledge in general* is based on – what entitles us to say that we know anything at all? These are the philosophical questions about the nature of knowledge. In this chapter we look at what it means to say that I know something, and how far this relates to ordinary managerial ideas about what is and can be known in and about organisations. The question of what specifically we know and what justifies us in saying so, we will look at in the following chapter, where we consider the practice that is generally thought most effective in leading to knowledge – scientific method.

First, what kinds of knowledge might we have, when considering management, business and organisations? Consider Box 4.1 below:

BOX 4.1

RECRUITING GRADUATE TRAINEES

A survey has found that students have strengths in terms of socialisation and humour, but lack key skills and qualities such as emotional resilience, managing their fears, and taking risks.

A study carried out for the accounting firm Ernst and Young indicated that only a quarter of students surveyed possessed the key qualities the firm required.

The research used a psychological assessment, and looked at a wide range of qualities relevant to work. It indicated that students were strong in areas such as problem solving and relationships, but lacked time management skills, were not strong in self-projection and dealing with personal reversals, and were weak at taking risks.

Source: BBC News, 11 February 2012

This is a typical example of research that is used to inform managerial practice. But how much confidence should we place in it? Does it tell us something fundamental about those individuals who were surveyed, or is the fact that someone is good at problem solving and building relationships a reflection of being a student, where solving problems is a key part of their day-to-day learning, and spending time with friends is part of the lifestyle? Further, is this true of students in general, or is it specific to those who choose to apply to a major accounting firm? And finally, how valid is the study anyway – might the students have been intimidated by the study, for example? Psychological assessment is not exactly like measuring people's heights – there is a significant level of statistical error that cannot be eradicated from the assessment instruments, as well as controversy about what they demonstrate.

None of this shows that the study is not valuable. It is simply to raise questions about exactly what we have come to know. It is to ask how sure we can be of the outcomes of the research. In other words, this material is persuasive but do we actually *know* what students are like as a result? Can we be *sure*?

In cases of large-scale disasters there are often subsequent enquiries. For example the American government published a major report identifying liability following the Deepwater Horizon disaster off the southern coast of the USA,[1] although in that report, the specific factors leading to the explosion

---

[1]The report is available at http://www.oilspillcommission.gov/final-report

were not conclusively established. One issue in reports of this kind is that information stemming from different kinds of source is involved, so there is a question of how it may be integrated. Where data from a measuring instrument that appears to read x is contradicted by a person's testimony that the reading never went above $x-5$, we assume that one or other piece of evidence is simply wrong. Human testimony is often assumed to be less reliable than scientific instrumentation or established theory.[2] But with scientific instruments there are potential inaccuracies: for example the phenomenon of 'noise' – randomly generated responses that do not represent genuine information. And where there is a conflict between pieces of evidence, some doubt attaches to each of them, even if experts accept one item as correct and the other as not so. However, even where there are no conflicts between items of evidence, the 'evidence' in front of you can be questioned – a meter reading, someone's testimony, or even a physical item. Is something genuinely a piece of burnt metal from a fire? Is someone's claim that they did not see something an indication that it was not there to see? Is a meter reading accurate or not?

So the main thing we can see with this example is that there are potential reasons to doubt what is being claimed. This is one of the very central philosophical issues in relation to knowledge: *almost all of it seems vulnerable to one kind of question or another.*

DOUBT, CERTAINTY AND KNOWLEDGE

4.2 This dubitable status of our knowledge was given perhaps its best known philosophical expression by the seventeenth-century French philosopher René Descartes. His argument, which is still debated today, was based on the idea that he decided to *actually* doubt anything that he *could* doubt, and see what was left. His view was that anything that could be doubted would not be certain knowledge but was only a belief – however strongly felt and strongly evidenced. This *method of doubt*, as Descartes called it, led him to question what he felt he knew from his education, from authorities and sources, and what he had accepted as common knowledge. Descartes then chose to doubt *anything he directly perceived*, in effect the whole world of the senses, arguing that even if he felt sure of what he perceived, an 'evil genius' might somehow have deceived his senses, leading him to dream such things as the seat he

---

[2]But there are many examples where the human got it right, such as Pliny the Younger's description of the volcanic eruption at Vesuvius in CE 79, which was assumed to have been fanciful rhetoric until the early 1980s, when it was realised that he had very accurately described what are now called pyroclastic flows of molten volcanic matter.

was sitting on, his feelings of pleasure, fatigue and so on. Many of us have, from time to time, lucid dreams that feel like the experiences we have when awake. So we cannot conclusively establish that any experience we are currently having is indeed the direct access to reality that we take it to be.

But does this argument prove that we know nothing? Not according to Descartes. He argued that if he was deceived then at least one thing exists – namely himself, if he is to say that he might have been deceived. If nothing else, he as a thinking being exists, else how could he think that something was or was not the case? This idea he summarised in the famous dictum 'cogito ergo sum' (I think therefore I am). And in this idea Descartes found the basis for reconstructing much of what he had doubted.

There is continuing debate as to exactly what Descartes' method of doubt, or his *cogito* dictum, really shows. True, he showed that we could cast doubt on any individual item of empirical knowledge. But it is not so clear that his argument shows that the whole external world could *collectively* be a deception. And equally, whilst the *cogito* may show that *something* exists, it is not clear that this is me, or that anything persists beyond the moments when doubt takes place. Nevertheless, as well as the legacy that doubt might undermine our belief in an external world – generally referred to as *philosophical scepticism* – which has remained a key issue for the philosophy of knowledge, Descartes also left the conviction that *something* can be found that represents certainty. And this conviction has remained a key aspiration for philosophers of knowledge.

A key assumption in Descartes' argument is that to know something is to be certain of it. Descartes argued that if there is any level of doubt then we cannot be certain of the item doubted, and therefore we cannot know it. One counter-argument to this is to point out that the feeling of certainty may be present or absent capriciously. I may be certain that a particular runner is going to win the Olympic gold medal. If that runner does win, we say "I *knew* it!" But in fact I did not have any special hold or access to the reality, I just had a feeling. Even with theoretical proofs in mathematics, we may feel certain of what is demonstrated, only for someone later to show that the proof is invalid.[3] So certainty does not look like a sufficient condition for knowledge.

Someone might object that even though certainty is not sufficient for knowledge, maybe it is necessary. However, consider a phenomenon seen with some TV quiz shows: someone is asked something and they give an instant – and correct – reaction, but immediately after this they express surprise that their answer is judged correct. It seems natural to say that the

---

[3]An interesting example of this are the 'proofs' of impossible results devised by Charles Dodgson (better known as Lewis Carroll) using clever, almost invisible, fallacies to prove things such as 1=2.

individual knows the answer, but is not certain of it. Someone might claim that after all the individual *was* certain of it, even if only briefly, but this seems to suggest that they *stopped* knowing it when they doubted their answer, which appears odd, as if we jump in and out of a state of knowing. And it would be implausible to deny that this is knowledge; in ordinary parlance answering a question correctly is taken as one of the best kinds of evidence that someone knew something.

In the world of business, our certainty that there is an external world, and that our senses provide us with good evidence of this, is so well grounded that to doubt it is generally out of the question. However, there are places where certainty and doubt are highly relevant to the question of what counts as business knowledge. As the Deepwater Horizon example mentioned earlier indicates, there can be times when a situation is so complex that it is not clear if we can place a reliance on *any* items presented to us.

Certainty, and presenting oneself confidently, are often seen as a virtue in business. However, one less desirable aspect of this is the temptation to present ideas as more strongly supported than they really are. There can be persuasive 'managerial' reasons to do so: for example, when there are limited financial resources to support projects, a manager may decide that admitting doubts about the project would only weaken the case for it, so the evidence for it is given in categorical, doubt-free, terms. But this is not a guide to what is true. It may have benefits such as being motivating for staff or convincing to investors. But it does not indicate that something is definitely the case.

So maybe we have to look elsewhere than in the experience of certainty for an understanding of what it is to know something, and correspondingly we need to find a different way to resolve the issue that any individual item that we experience may be doubted.

KNOWLEDGE AND BELIEF

4.3 We have seen that Descartes used the idea that knowledge was immune from doubt to try to clarify what he actually knew. His argument implies we could not know for sure anything in the external world that we access through our senses,[4] but that we could be sure about at least some elements of our personal experience. This idea that knowledge must be certain does not, however, fit with our characteristic views of what we know: in ordinary life we feel that we do know things about the world we contact through our senses – indeed for many people this is the

---

[4]In fact Descartes, following his doubt and *cogito* arguments, did make efforts to prove that the external world could be known, but his arguments to support this are not generally seen as valid.

best example of knowledge, not the least. We shall turn now to a different approach, based on the relationship between knowledge and belief.

BOX 4.2

DIFFERENT LEVELS OF CONFIDENCE

In the strategy meeting the marketing director had argued that a rebrand was essential, despite the doubts of the chief accountant. Whilst the operations manager was in favour, he had some worries about the resources needed.

The CEO started to sum up: 'Right, what do we really know here? It's clear that we are losing sales to the competition, and it seems to be because of poor after-sales service.'

The marketing director interrupted: 'It's not that it seems to be this, we know this is the problem.'

The CEO responded: 'Well, you believe this pretty strongly, but there might be other factors involved as well.'

'We've got a whole lot of evidence here, the focus groups and surveys, that justify my view.'

'Like all the justification you had last year, to launch a youth version of the product? That cost us hundreds of thousands,' responded the chief accountant.

'You'll see, I'm right, I know I am,' retorted the marketing director.

If we analyse the situation presented in Box 4.2, we see the following:

- the loss of sales, and the idea that poor after-sales service plays some part in the loss of sales, are agreed by all;
- the marketing director believes that after-sales service is the main factor in the loss of sales, and claims the evidence of focus groups and surveys as his justification for this;
- the chief accountant points out that a justified belief can still be wrong.

We see here *evidence* as a key element in understanding what knowledge is. Not that Descartes dismissed the importance of evidence. But he did not regard it as being part of the *definition* of knowledge. Now, note the point of the chief accountant's comment: it is not enough that someone's belief is justified – things that are justified can still be false. So the belief has to be true, as well as justified. This idea of knowledge goes back to Plato, in his dialogue *Theatetus*. It seems to capture that special connection that knowledge has with the truth by using the idea of *justification* as the vehicle for this.

On this view then, I can be said to know something if:

a I believe it
b it is true
c I have some appropriate form of justification for believing it.

This view of knowledge takes the concept away from a simple experience or feeling of certainty, as it links the state that someone is in to the external fact of whether what they believe is true or not. So someone cannot directly distinguish between those things they know and those things they believe with a good degree of justification but happen to be wrong about. Still, the best kind of test we can have of knowledge is the evidence we have for believing it. Now, there are certain levels of confidence and evidence built into this view. It is not simply the case that *any* level of justification or belief is a mark of knowledge, as Box 4.3 illustrates.

BOX 4.3

Consider a contested copyright claim between two firms, A and B. The final judgment in a case of this kind is generally based on *the balance of probabilities*. As a result of the legal judgment we may well come to believe that it is company A, and we may have a list of factors that justify our view, and it may be true that A originally owned the copyright (whether we have access to the fact or not). So we have all the components of this definition of knowledge as justified true belief.

But we may have also heard arguments that counter this, so there may remain questions. Two people could therefore conclude as follows:

- one might say 'On the basis of the arguments I believe that A owned the copyright, though I am not completely confident about this'
- the other might say 'On the basis of the arguments I am completely confident that A is the owner of the copyright'

Although in the previous section we saw that the experience of believing with certainty is neither necessary nor sufficient, in the illustration given in Box 4.3 it does seem that each of these parties are in possession of the same considerations (and thus have the same logical justification) and both believe that A owns the copyright, it nevertheless seems that their confidence in the judgment differs. Therefore it seems odd to say that they are both in the same state of knowledge. So if we are actually to say that justified true belief is knowledge, we have to make some assumptions about the quality of the justification that is given for the belief.

However, there is an even more difficult counter-example to the idea that justified true belief constitutes knowledge. In a famous article Edmund Gettier[5] demonstrated that there can be cases where someone believes something, it is true, and they have what appears to be an excellent justification for their belief, and yet unequivocally they do not know it.

BOX 4.4

A 'GETTIER' EXAMPLE

The Chief Executive's PA is asked to check the petty cash box, and finds that there is £47.50 there.

A short while later, they are asked if there is enough money in the box to pay £40 for sending a parcel by courier. The PA answers truly 'Yes'. If challenged on what basis they know this, they can answer truly that they checked the box only that morning. So the PA believes that there is more than £40 in the petty cash box, and this is true, and they have a good justification for saying this.

BUT – unbeknown to the PA, a colleague borrowed £30 from the box, popped out of the office to buy a present for her daughter, but could not find what she wanted, so returned the money before anyone noticed.

A range of similar counter-examples has been constructed with this idea of interrupting the 'justification' factors but restoring the factual truth that is believed, so that these are called by the collective term '*Gettier examples*'. One way round this is to say that there needs to be a continuity between the fact believed and the individual's reasons for believing it. In the PA case the continuity has been violated, so one could say that this is after all not a justified true belief in the sense required for knowledge. This has led to a *causal* theory of knowledge – that somehow the thread between a fact and someone who is said to know it must involve a causal chain that preserves the truth. Consider perception as a source of knowledge. In certain circumstances (e.g. the presence of distorting mirrors) perception may be fallible, but if there is a clear chain from object to perceiver that is not interrupted then we can say, for example, I know that the vase in front of me is conical, because I can see it is.

But this is not the final word on this view. We need to have a clear understanding of which causal processes preserve knowledge and which ones do not. Seeing the vase through a window presumably preserves knowledge.

---

[5]E. L. Gettier (1963) 'Is Justified True Belief Knowledge?'. *Analysis*, 23: 121–3. A terrific example of how a powerful idea can be expressed with brevity – the article is less than three full pages long.

Does seeing it through a web-cam? Perhaps, though assumptions have to be made that the processing and transmission that the web-cam involves preserves the truth of what is perceived. Suppose the web-cam accidentally turns the image into a negative – in the case of the vase we might accept that the visual information is the same and that therefore someone still knows what the vase looks like – but in a more complicated image such as a picture of a football match we might feel less inclined to say this. The point here is that we have to make assumptions before we can say that a certain causal linkage is sufficient to turn a true belief into the right kind of justified true belief.

In this section we have seen the potential but also the shortcomings of the theory that knowledge is a justified true belief. The essence of that feeling of what it is to know something still seems to have eluded both the discussion of justification as well as the earlier one of the experience of being certain. In the next section we will look at a different aspect of our knowledge, namely the metaphor of it as a co-ordinated whole, possessing foundations on which an edifice of thought is built.

THE IDEA OF A FOUNDATION OF KNOWLEDGE

4.4

Descartes started by doubting things because he wanted to find something that was absolutely certain, which would then operate as a foundation on which knowledge could be based. Though his own attempts to build this were not generally seen as successful[6] his strategy – to find something that is rock-solid knowledge and then use it as the starting point for drawing conclusions about what else we know – has been extremely influential. Indeed much philosophical work that has followed Descartes has been an attempt in one way or another to find such a foundation.

At first sight the issue of how and why our knowledge has a foundation may seem not especially relevant to business; after all, if there is a problem with our overall corpus of knowledge then this makes everything, not just business, questionable. However, modern business is based on a huge volume of technology, itself derived from the many advances in scientific knowledge achieved over the last four centuries. Most of the knowledge that we use, whether critically or uncritically, is *inferred* – that is, drawn as conclusions from earlier knowledge. And that earlier knowledge in turn is most likely to be inferred from other knowledge, and so on. So understanding where it all starts is important for understanding what our present state of knowledge is. As an illustration, look at Box 4.5:

---

[6]He argued that anything that we perceived *clearly and distinctly* had to be true, though this claim ended up being dependent on rather special senses of these terms.

BOX 4.5

Consider the finances of a large firm. There will probably be reserves that the firm keeps reasonably liquid – quick to turn into cash should there be an urgent need. One way to do this is to hold short-term securities such as currency derivatives. In doing this, a huge raft of electronic, economic and mathematico-logical knowledge is brought to bear on the matter, in the form of 'expert systems', economic software packages to evaluate market trends and make trades.

Take the logical knowledge involved in this: the original developers of electronic computing (such as Alan Turing) drew on work done by Bertrand Russell and Gottlob Frege on systems of inference, but they drew in turn on the work of others such as Augustus de Morgan, Leibniz and Newton. If doubt were thrown on our current understanding of those systems of mathematical logic then the results of those financial analysis packages would be themselves doubtful, whatever their apparently successful results.

Similarly, the hardware is based on a wide range of contributory elements of electronics, chemistry, materials science. Take just one of these – high-speed computing in part involves calculations of speeds of electricity and electro-magnetic radiation (light) in certain materials, and the capacity of wires and fibres to carry signals successfully. If we were to discover, for example, that such radiation did not always behave the way we expect it to, then the structure of computing as we currently utilise it could be put into question.

Box 4.5 indicates that our knowledge is built upon other items of knowledge, which in turn have some supporting basis. In general most of what we take as knowledge is based on something else. Think of the process of repeatedly questioning something that we claim to know: I know that this software program will help me calculate financial returns, because of the logical and electronic knowledge that has been used to develop it; I know the electronic knowledge because it rests on sound experiments conducted by this or that scientist; I know that the methods used by the scientist are sound because ... and so on.

The idea behind foundationalism is that such a chain of reasons needs to stop somewhere. Otherwise we would have an *infinite regress* – an unending sequence of reasoning – which would mean that we cannot completely resolve the sources of our knowledge. Repeated 'why' questioning can always be raised of any supporting statement, until we get to an answer which cannot be doubted. And at that point we will have certain knowledge.

Following Descartes, two competing traditions tried to establish a foundation of this kind for our knowledge of the physical world, in one case in the very concepts we use to frame our ideas, from which we could derive our knowledge using pure reason (as a result they were called the *rationalists*) and in the other case in the most basic sensory experiences we have (called *empiricists*). In their pure form both these approaches were strongly critiqued by the work of Immanuel Kant, who showed that knowledge arises from a combination of thought and experience,[7] though strands of rationalist thinking, and more so of empiricism, have persisted since that time in modified forms.

Since Kant, empiricists have continued to present knowledge as built on the foundations of our most fundamental sensory experiences. However, it has proved impossible to clearly define a fundamental sense experience. Attempts have been made to analyse knowledge about, say, physical objects, into complex combinations of potential sense experiences – so that the concept of 'table' is reduced to a series of statements about what one might see, hear, feel, touch etc. However, even calling something a red square introduces more than just 'pure' experience, for we already have done some processing on it to categorise it as red, and as having a certain definite shape (so it is not yet at the most basic level, but at some remove from that). Furthermore, these very basic sensory experiences still do not capture the richness of our knowledge of objects. Our intuitive understanding of the difference between a shiny table and a reflection from a mirror is immediate and uncomplicated, whereas the attempt to define this difference in terms of the most fundamental items we might or see, touch etc. would need to be excessively complex. Whilst this is not a killer objection to the idea that our knowledge may be built up from our experience, it makes it more problematic than we would expect such 'ordinary' knowledge to be.[8]

To the fundamental issue of Descartes' doubt, it seems that the foundationalist does not have a completely watertight response. In the next section we will look at an approach that does away with the idea of a solid single basis.

---

[7] It would be impossible to summarise Kant's arguments and do sufficient justice to them without writing an entire book devoted solely to that end. But essentially he argued that although our knowledge of the external world comes from our contact with it via experience (so the empiricists were right on that count) the form in which we have experiences is determined by structural features necessary for any mind to be able to think and have experience in the way we do (so the rationalists were right about that aspect).

[8] This difficulty with specifying experiences that would form the foundation of knowledge has led some to look at the question the other way round, and explain our knowledge of the world as a result of the world we are in: in other words, the world is of a kind to support our having these beliefs. However, this *external* foundationalist view does not resolve the problem of how I can separate out what I know from what I believe strongly but am wrong about.

BOX 4.6

The western approach to medical knowledge and practice is characterised by paying attention to cellular bio-chemistry. Chinese medicine is based on a theory of energy channels, and homeopathy categorises treatments in terms of sameness or difference.

Whilst none of the three approaches mentioned enjoys unequivocal success, it is still arguable that none is clearly baseless – each has adherents who claim that it has successfully treated conditions in patients. Equally, each has had its share of failures.

None of these three is reducible to any of the others theoretically. Nor has any (so far) been dismissed as illusory (though there is controversy over the claims of homeopathy). Each has its own conceptual framework, and its own explanations of its successes and failures.

KNOWLEDGE AS A COHERENT SYSTEM

4.5 Given the difficulty of finding something that will be both acceptable as a genuine foundation, *and* substantial enough to help us infer what we generally think of as knowledge, some philosophers have looked at an alternative approach that rests on the idea that our knowledge forms a *coherent whole* – and hence this idea of coherence is the principal rationale for our confidence in what we know.

In Box 4.6 the three kinds of medicine outlined are for all practical purposes distinct, almost competing, forms of medical science and practice. And whilst most western medical practitioners and researchers would emphasise the primacy of their bio-chemical conception, this is not seen by adherents of Chinese or homeopathic medicine as refuting their approaches. Arguably, then, we could say that there are three coherent but distinct belief systems with respect to medicine.

The point about Box 4.6 goes beyond the claim that there are different systems of medicine that make their own claims to knowledge, still less that they are of equal value when it comes to the effects of treatment. It is rather that as systems of thinking each forms a whole that has a certain kind of inner *coherence*, a kind of integration of the different components.

Now whilst one might reject any individual element of each of these systems of thought, this is not a simple subtraction of a statement from the stock of knowledge, but requires the *systemic* adjustment of a number of elements. So, for example, if we came to reject the practice of radiation treatment for some cancer patients, this would probably come, not *simply* from poor results[9] but from when these lead to a rethinking of how cancerous cells respond to radiation, how the body reacts to radiation and so on. One item of knowledge does not exist in isolation, but as part of a network, a 'web of belief' as the American philosopher Quine described it, a *raft* of knowledge, where no one piece stands on its own in isolation.[10] This contrasts with foundationalism, where some things can be identified and accepted as independent of others. The coherence view of knowledge does not deny the importance of our senses as key sources of knowledge. But it does not analyse empirical knowledge as all logically derived from combinations of claims such as 'I see a red square here now, and a blue circle there' etc. Rather the coherence view presents our knowledge as a whole, that has a certain degree of coherence to it.

How beliefs are accepted or rejected is based on the *fit* of new discoveries with what we already accept. Suppose someone proposed a new principle of advertising, that claimed success by making people feel ill when they thought they would be deprived of a certain product. This contradicts the generally accepted view that promotion should focus on the benefits of having a product, using positive messages to associate the product with happiness. If marketing strategies based on this new approach failed to achieve positive results then it would be swiftly rejected. But even if there were positive results it would not be *immediately* accepted – alternative explanations that were more compatible with existing marketing theory would be considered first. Only as the existing network of knowledge proved flexible enough to accommodate the new idea would it be (gradually) accepted.

Some ideas may be easier to replace than others – so a particular claim about a specific marketing tactic may require fewer adjustments than, say, general theories of customer behaviour, on which a lot of other knowledge is based. But any element is fallible in principle. This contrasts with the foundational approach, where the fundamental building blocks of knowledge are certain facts. The process by which items are included or replaced in a knowledge network rests on the idea that human beings will seek to have the simplest, most elegant explanations that are compatible with the evidence. If one belief system is simpler than another then it will resist replacement

---

[9]Though it would probably only be due to continuing poor results that one would come to question the treatment. However, it is notable how long certain practices can continue to find favour despite low success rates.

[10]The raft metaphor was popularised by E. Sosa in his (1980) article 'The Raft and the Pyramid: Coherence versus Foundations in the Theory of Knowledge', *Midwest Studies in Philosophy*, 5: 3–25 – the raft being coherence-based approaches, and the pyramid representing the foundational view. Quine used his metaphor in a ground-breaking (1951) article 'Two Dogmas of Empiricism', *The Philosophical Review*, 60: 20–43.

by the latter, unless there is substantial evidence supporting the new idea – which in itself reduces the general coherence of the system.

But a much more controversial consequence of the coherence approach is that *there can be more than one equally plausible overall network of knowledge*. One such network cannot be critically evaluated from the perspective of another, as the illustration of different medical traditions indicates. And in turn this suggests that no one network could be conclusively demonstrated to be superior to others. Hence it would seem that there can be multiple and incommensurably different conceptions of reality. Although we generally assume that there is a single external world, of which, over time, we can slowly improve our knowledge, the coherence view is compatible with belief systems that conflict with others, but is not subject to external criticism. This undermines the idea of knowledge as the outcome of a gradual, unified and *collective* process of conceptual growth. However, in the next chapter we shall see that it has had support from many management researchers.

SUMMARY

This chapter has covered some of the key classical issues in epistemology: how much can be doubted, what can we know for sure, is knowledge justified true belief, and what are the respective features and merits of looking at knowledge in terms of foundations or in terms of integration.

One point that emerges from this discussion is that the moves that we have characterised as typical of either a foundationalist or a coherentist, are in fact *things that we would naturally do on occasion as part of our natural knowledge-seeking activity*. When considering what we know, we will look to what we think is a basis for that knowledge, as well as think about how our beliefs fit together. And when faced with apparently conflicting evidence we are as likely to consider the robustness of that evidence as we are to see if other related beliefs need adjustment. We do not adopt a single mono-thematic approach. Perhaps the 'problem' of knowledge lies less with the status of our knowledge than with the willingness of philosophers to take ideas such as foundational certainty or the interdependence of beliefs beyond their limits.

QUESTIONS FOR CONSOLIDATION

1 What would be the main points of dispute with the results of a management survey?

2 How would you see the idea that knowledge should have a sure foundation affecting the manner in which modern operational management systems such as JIT are understood?

3 How might you argue with someone who claimed that the expert software system they had developed, based on advanced mathematical concepts such as fractals and eigenvalues, could guarantee at least 99.5% accuracy in predicting the rise or fall of certain categories of investment?

FURTHER READING

Audi, R. *Epistemology*, 3rd edn (Routledge, 2010), Chs 10, 11, 13.
Descartes, R. *Meditations and Other Metaphysical Writings* (Penguin Classics, 1998, trans. D. Clarke).
O'Brien, D. *An Introduction to the Theory of Knowledge* (Polity Press, 2006), Chs 6–9.
Plato, *Theatetus* (Penguin Classics, 1987 trans. R. Waterfield).

KNOWLEDGE IN MANAGEMENT – SOME ANSWERS

5

After reading this chapter you should be able to:

- Analyse component elements in examples of organisational knowledge
- Identify key features of approaches to knowledge such as critical realism, or positivism
- Critically identify arguments rejecting modernism as a basis for knowledge about management.

In the previous chapter we noted the distinction between foundationalist and coherentist views of knowledge. The foundationalist lays emphasis on the idea that knowledge should be built on a sure basis, on which the 'pyramid' of all our knowledge rests. In contrast the coherentist emphasises the idea that knowledge has to fit together – we could not have an item of knowledge that was entirely independent of everything else we knew. This distinction remains a significant backdrop to the arguments in this chapter.

EMPIRICAL AND NON-EMPIRICAL ELEMENTS IN KNOWLEDGE

5.1 Return to the rationalist-empiricist debate. That debate, carried out mostly between the time of René Descartes and Immanuel Kant, focused on the ultimate source of our knowledge of the world around us. The empiricists argued that apart from logic and mathematics, everything we know about the world is derived from the experience of our senses. In contrast the rationalists argued that our knowledge of the world is founded on our understanding. After Kant, most philosophers have tended to accept that some element of both sense experience and understanding is required for someone to gain knowledge, even though some still lean more towards the empirical and others the rational.

The rationalist-empiricist debate has an echo in alternative approaches to management research, contrasting quantitative with qualitative (sometimes called interpretavist) approaches. In this chapter we will consider the question as to what knowledge at all is possible with respect to organisations. We will focus in the main on those approaches that attempt to mirror natural science. Most people would take science to be about as good a source of knowledge as we have. Whilst this view might be contestable, it remains the case that natural science is generally accepted by most of us as having led to a vast increase in our knowledge of the world about us.

BOX 5.1

It is generally held in investment circles that bio-technology can yield good investment returns. Interest in improving health and well-being often leads to high sales of products such as new treatments, or pain relief. So when researchers working for Casterbridge Healthcare published scientific papers that identified promising results with a new method of protecting against 'standard' infections of childhood such as measles or chickenpox, this excited great interest in the financial markets. 'A step beyond vaccination' was how one analyst expressed it, and the share price of the firm tripled overnight.

Three years later, there was still no progress towards a marketable treatment based on the 'discovery'. Trials with human subjects had not been successful, and other research teams had not achieved the same scale of results that the Casterbridge team had claimed.

The company was virtually bankrupt, and only avoided closure due to the recent award of a new contract by a Middle-Eastern government, for supplies of an existing product.

By this time the share price was 3p, from a high three years previously of £6.49. Several major investment houses experienced losses. However, one well-known investor, Nicholas de Varrance, had made a success of his investment, buying shares when the original report was published, and selling almost at the very top of the market.

'No one knows the pharmaceuticals investment market as well as Varrance' cooed one financial journalist. He bragged 'I knew that this was not the golden goose some people thought it was. These medical advances never are.'

In Box 5.1 there are several possible areas of knowledge:

- 'common knowledge' about the investment potential of medical advances
- knowledge embodied in the scientific research papers
- the knowledge of the financial trader.

One first question here is what exactly is 'well known' about medical advances? This is not a direct cause-and-effect link. Amongst other things there is a wide range of contextual circumstances that underpin a link between medical advance and investment success. A further issue is the generalisability of the belief that medical advances are a good investment. If historical data concerning previous announcements is to be generalisable to future cases, then we need to determine how significant are the differences between cases: the researchers may have discovered a greater or lower level of correlation, or used a different medium for injection, and so on. So when evaluating what we know in a situation such as this, we have to *decide* whether a certain difference matters in terms of its impact on knowledge. This decision in itself cannot be based solely on the empirical evidence.

When we turn to the knowledge of the financial trader, we should distinguish between knowledge that can be expressed as a statement (sometimes referred to as *knowing that,* or propositional knowledge) and skills based knowledge (*knowing how*). In this case however the distinction is not as clear cut as, say, the difference between knowing how to ride a bicycle and knowing that the bicycle will only move if the wheels turn around. The financial trader uses some propositional knowledge – for example knowledge of mathematical formulae. But it is not simply a matter of knowing what the formula is and what values to input to it. The trader also needs to understand the limits of its applicability, the most volatile components, the variables that can be stated with most confidence, and so on. The context in which the formula appears will influence the trader in deciding how much reliance to place on the results. So over and above the knowledge and skill embodied in their decisions, traders use their *judgement* as to how best to apply the formula. This is a common issue with applied knowledge such as financial models or engineering technology – textbook answers sometimes do not work, for unknown reasons, but the effective professional uses their judgement to determine when this is the case and respond accordingly.

Another aspect of practical knowledge is *heuristic principles.* For example, in the management of major emergencies, energy installations work on the basis that normally only one major system failure will occur at a time – the chance of two fundamental failures is so remote as not to merit consideration. This is not a piece of general knowledge, of a form such as 'all cases of *x* are also cases of *y*.' So in the simple explanation of propositional knowledge as being 'knowing that' it seems not to fit.[1] However, there is something 'propositional' about it, in the sense that it involves the individual having some kind of content that they hold in their mind, as it were.

Like the 'knowledge' of the financial trader discussed earlier, this content seems to suggest certain conclusions, without giving a determinate

---

[1] It is perhaps even more clearly not a case of knowing how.

answer. It is natural to describe this as knowledge, even though one might qualify it by adding that someone needs to understand when to apply such knowledge.

Again, *judgement* as to when this principle is appropriate, and when to overlook it, is crucial. Consider the case of a major manufacturing accident, say where one set of control data seems to indicate one problem, and a different set of data seems to indicate another. The 'one system failure at a time' guide would suggest that one set of data was misleading, perhaps due to faulty collection (say that an electrical dial was malfunctioning). But there remains the risk that in fact the two apparently conflicting sets of performance data are both correct, and there are two different faults that have developed simultaneously. An experienced operator may have an inkling of this and decide that there are in fact two problems, not one. In such a situation we would say that the 'knowledge' that systems do not produce more than one fault at a time requires judgement to decide whether it applies.

So one lesson to draw is that in our day-to-day life, questions of knowledge rarely present themselves in pure forms. There are some items that could be candidates for knowledge, some that are too vague to have the status of clear evidence-based knowledge, some that are no more than well supported beliefs, and other items that are best seen as rules of thumb.

In the next section we will look at a characteristic distinction made between two different forms of empiricism, as these apply to organisational knowledge.

POSITIVIST AND REALIST VIEWS OF KNOWLEDGE IN ORGANISATIONS

5.2 Both of the terms 'positivism' and 'realism' have been used very widely in differing contexts, in philosophy, in sociology, and elsewhere, so that it can be hard to isolate a core sense that underlies all of these uses. Indeed, if one reads the great positivists of the nineteenth and twentieth centuries, it is difficult to reconcile everything they claim.[2] Inevitably, then, what follows is a particular interpretation of the idea.

Positivism may be best understood as a version of empiricism that claims that our knowledge of the external world is purely what we gain from our senses. Empiricism in general is the view that our knowledge is *grounded* on what we gain from our senses, whilst positivism goes further and claims

---

[2]The term was coined by August Comte in the 1830s. He used this as the basis for an explanation of the different disciplines of knowledge. Others took aspects of Comte's ideas in different directions: Durkheim advocated an empirical form of sociology, Mill an empiricist philosophy of science, and later the logical positivists argued that all our language referred to sensory data alone.

that what we gain from our senses *is* what we know. Those empiricists who are not positivists hold that while our knowledge is *based* on what we experience, there may be elements of that knowledge that go beyond our experience. A positivist however insists that there is no knowledge (apart from pure logic and its derivative, mathematics) that is not directly made up of what we experience from our senses.

In organisational terms positivism suggests that when we talk of, say, a firm's strategy, this is to be explained, ultimately, in terms of what is directly observable – the documents, the stated intentions, the behaviours. *Interior,* non-observable elements, such as the meaning that someone attaches to a particular statement, are only acceptable if they can be recast as statements about behaviour, in other words reframed as covertly composed of observables.

In contrast, a *realist* view of an organisation does not try to force every element into an observable interpretation. Although it still holds to the empiricist attitude that experience is the source of our knowledge, it accepts that some parts may resist empirical investigation. The realist may accept that the collection of documents, managers' announcements, and behaviours is all that we can look at to establish a firm's strategy. But they recognise that this may not be sufficient to provide a complete account of the strategy. Experience is all we have to guide our knowledge, but some aspects of that knowledge escape experience.

In some ways this difference is analogous to a difference between the views of some of the philosophers of the seventeenth and eighteenth centuries. Bishop Berkeley was a phenomenalist – arguing that not only our knowledge, but also all existence, was composed solely of sense perceptions. In contrast, Kant, although accepting that all our knowledge was grounded in experience, nevertheless accepted that some of it went beyond that. It would be stretching the analogy to state that this is the same as the difference between positivism and realism, but the main idea is similar – that in one case experience is everything we know, whilst in the other it is the source, but not the entirety, of our knowledge. As with those debates, this is as much about ontology – what there is – as it is about what we know. The positivist claims that our world is composed solely of observable items. As far as knowledge about organisations is concerned this would mean that we could in theory directly experience every aspect of an organisation, whereas a realist view leaves open the possibility that we might not be able to access via our senses some elements of what we know.

However, what does the realist claim might not be completely explained by experience? A key aspect of this is the idea of something being possible 'in principle': in practice we probably will never get to observe directly what the centre of the sun is like, but we can still imagine what we might observe when there – great heat, swirling gases, and so on. In contrast, we could not possibly ever identify the final ten digits of the number π. Being an unending decimal, in principle π cannot be completely determined. It is important to note that the positivist does not claim that everything actually *is* observable. Some things are just too difficult to get to – the centre of the sun, or people's deepest anxieties. But that does not make them in principle unobservable, just practically so.

Kant however argued that there were elements of reality that *in principle* could not be accessed via our senses – he distinguished between things as they appeared to us (he used the term *phenomena* for these) and things as they were in themselves (which he called *noumena*): the only thing we knew about the latter was that in some way they were the ground, the basis for how things appeared to us, but beyond that there was nothing we could say. There are points where some modern realists seem to argue something similar – not so much in terms of noumena but in terms of the idea that what we observe cannot capture the whole of what we mean when we talk about, say, communities, or cultures.

The difference between these approaches for understanding organisations is illustrated in Box 5.2

BOX 5.2

'THE WAY WE DO THINGS ROUND HERE'

When John started his new job, he needed time to settle into it. Once he had learnt the formal procedures, there was a period of understanding other issues: which senior managers to confide in, which processes to do properly, and which rules could be broken or even ignored. At first these seemed arbitrary, but over time he slowly gained a 'feel' for why things worked in that particular way, and after a while it came to feel quite natural.

One way to explain this is to say that John has learnt the culture by making sense of a series of clues and patterns, in the context of his existing beliefs and attitudes. Another is to say that really John did not 'learn' the firm's culture intellectually but rather he came to 'live' it. In coming to understand how that particular organisation worked John had to feel the norms and expressed values in the context of the activities and emotions of members of the community in question – in fact he *became* such a member.

The former can be given a positivist interpretation – that one observes a range of phenomena and comes to explain or understand them in terms of theoretical constructs. In contrast the second kind of account appears to be saying that observation on its own cannot be the basis for understanding a culture, and that part of that meaning is only accessible by how we live. Arguably, this is a realist perspective, suggesting that the 'living' bit in our knowledge is not reducible to accounts of what we gain from our senses.

There are problems with both positivism and realism. When we say 'CNN is more adventurous than the BBC' the positivist would need to say that 'CNN' is a shorthand for a complex set of statements about what one might perceive if one read certain documents, entered one of the firm's buildings etc. One puzzle is that this makes something apparently simple look very complicated. But what is more difficult for the positivist is why one particular set of such actual or predicted observations can be called 'CNN' and some other set is simply a random collection of such perceptions.[3] Why not add other perceptions into the definition of 'CNN'?

For the realist this is not a problem – they would explain that one particular set of actual or possible perceptions just *is* what we call CNN, because this refers to something over and above those perceptions themselves – namely the real thing CNN, which is the basic ground that entitles us to regard some set of perceptions as unified, as opposed to it being just a stray grouping of components. The positivist's focus on phenomena seems to leave out the sense of something underlying those phenomena that pulls it all together, so that we are not just perceiving a stream of events: rather we are having *different experiences of* CNN. In some way we posit that there is something *behind* all these phenomena that justifies us calling them perceptions or experiences of that company. Without this, there is no explanation for why we think in terms of objects, be these social ones such as organisations, or physical ones such as pineapples, at all.

But there is a difficulty also with the realist position. If, as has been argued above, we have to project some underlying reality in order to be able to make sense of the many perceptions and experiences we have, then what *is* this underlying reality? What is the basis of the underlying ground of experience that the realist refers to? By definition, it is not itself something perceivable. The underpinning 'reality' of CNN, then, is something we assume but cannot observe. Not that this refutes realism, but it does make clear that this does not provide a complete explanation of what we know and how it relates to what we can observe.

THE POPPER–KUHN DEBATE

5.3 We now will turn to a different aspect of the question of knowledge in management. Perhaps the best claims to knowledge are those based on scientific investigation. We shall look therefore at science as a source of knowledge, starting with natural science, making the assumption that this analysis can be applied to knowledge of social phenomena such as organisational life.

---

[3]This echoes the theory of nominal definition, and the idea that a term or idea can be explained solely on the basis of a particular collection of components.

Karl Popper was a leading philosopher of science in the twentieth century. His ideas, revolutionary at first, have become a cornerstone of contemporary thinking about how science can lead to knowledge. Like many thinkers, his ideas evolved over time, so that what he argued in his early career was not always consistent with what he believed in later life, though there is a common theme running through much of this work.

At the start of Popper's career, the philosophy of science was dominated by a concept known as *inductivism*. This held that we gain knowledge of the empirical world by building up ever greater volumes of data to support our theories – the more evidence we have the better the support. But when Popper looked at how scientists actually went about their work, he saw a different phenomenon. Instead of collecting more evidence, scientists designed critical tests of their theories, picking out the most difficult situations, to see if the theories held in all cases. However much confirming evidence might have been built up, a few key tests that disconfirmed a theory could refute it.

Popper was greatly impressed by Einstein's Theory of Relativity, especially inspired by the fact that this implied a surprising, and quite unexpected, prediction about how observers would see the solar eclipse in 1919. As this prediction ran counter to what the orthodoxy on light implied, it became a crucial test of the theory. In the event Einstein's prediction was fulfilled, and this was a major step in the theory, despite its great abstraction, being accepted by the scientific community.

Popper also recognised that Einstein's prediction was a *demanding* test of his theory: if the theory passed this then its claim to be true was much stronger. Popper thus came to the view that scientific theories are tested not by the accumulation of data, but *by efforts to refute* them. The scientist makes a hypothesis, and identifies what this new approach predicts. If any of the predictions are not fulfilled then the theory is rejected. If they all are fulfilled, that does not demonstrate that the theory was true, only that it had shown itself to be acceptable for the moment. Scientists would continue a further testing of the theory; only after a process of rigorous testing would a theory eventually be accepted, though never absolutely.

Popper's view of scientific knowledge is generally known as *hypothetico-deductivism*: it starts with a hypothesis, and proceeds by deducing what that implies.[4] He went further to argue that theories which tried to insulate themselves from refutation were not really scientific at all. In particular, certain social and psychological theories such as Marxism and Freudianism were criticised by Popper as *pseudo-science*, because they purported to be scientific but in fact built in mechanisms to subsume evidence that appeared

---

[4] It is also sometimes associated with the phrase 'conjecture and refutation' which afforded the basis for one of Popper's books. Popper's ideas were presaged by the nineteenth-century writer, William Whewell.

to refute them.[5] For Popper the possibility of refutation is central to a scientific statement: they had to be *falsifiable* – open to the possibility that they might be refuted – in order to be seen as making a substantial claim about the world.

In contrast, Thomas Kuhn argued that as science progresses, it *oscillates* between two different kinds of intellectual condition. In *normal science*, investigation in any particular discipline is dominated by a theoretical template, which he called a *paradigm*. An example of these might be the theory of evolution in biological theory. Such paradigms embody fundamental assumptions made by researchers whose work is mainly elaborating the paradigm in more detail. Eventually however, puzzles appear which cannot be explained, and these anomalies grow in importance until the paradigm is no longer useful. We then enter into what Kuhn called *revolutionary science*, where there is no guiding theoretical framework, and Popperian-style conjecture and refutation is a critical element in progressing towards a new paradigm. After a period of theoretical anarchy, a new theory is proposed which appears to solve most of the key current problems; this becomes installed as a new paradigm, the research returns to a 'normal' situation, and the cycle repeats.

Whilst some aspects of the differences between Kuhn and Popper can be exaggerated, there is at least one key contrast. For Popper, science was a unified body of knowledge, where researchers were in effect a single community, following commonly recognised lines of enquiry to test theories, and eventually arriving at a consensus as to whether a theory is refuted or has so far resisted such efforts. For Kuhn it was theoretically possible for there to be competing paradigms, with the effect that no one paradigm might be provably superior to another.[6] Whilst Kuhn himself rejected the charge of *relativism* (the idea that that different communities have their own unique kinds of knowledge that are equally valid) many people used his views to support such arguments.

BOX 5.3

INVESTIGATING THE AFFLUENT WORKER:
A CASE OF HYPOTHETICO-DEDUCTIVISM?

In the 1960s, as British workers started earning higher wages, it was thought that as they became more affluent they might lose their working-class roots and become more akin to the middle classes: a phenomenon known at the time as *'embourgeoisement'*. A team of researchers led by two Oxford academics, Goldthorpe and Lockwood, interviewed a sample

---

[5]Though this view continues to be debated.

[6]A feature developed further by the philosopher Paul Feyerabend.

of car workers based in southern England who fell into this category of being 'blue collar' but with rising earning capacity. They found that the workers retained their working-class attitudes. So the thesis of embourgeoisement was at that time refuted.

Although Goldthorpe and Lockwood did not explicitly model their study on a Popperian model, it can be analysed along these lines. From the hypothesis (*embourgeoisement*) are deduced a series of predictions – the expected responses that the workers would have made to the questions put to them in their interviews, following which interviews are conducted and what is said is recorded (observed). The results conflict with the predictions as to what the workers would have said if *embourgeoisement* were true, so the theory is rejected.

The idea that there can be alternative paradigms, neither of which can be used as the basis for refuting the other, takes us back to the examples of different kinds of medicine discussed in the previous chapter. Whilst relativism does not find many adherents in respect of natural science, it has been influential in some schools of social science, and especially with anti-realist approaches such as postmodernism and critical theory.

However, there were areas where Popper and Kuhn were in agreement. Both of them argued that science is not a mechanism that drives us inexorably upwards to bigger truths about our world. Rather, it proceeds as much by discontinuity as by gradual accretions of evidence. Further, for both Popper and Kuhn truth is never completely established – *the behaviour of scientists* in deciding to accept or reject theories is a critical variable, not entirely determined by the evidence. In other words, there is an element of subjectivity even with natural science.

The pure foundational approach to knowledge, as discussed in the previous chapter, is not easy to make compatible with either of these views. Granted, in principle on Popper's view it is possible to erect a 'pyramid' of knowledge claims each resting on earlier more fundamental ones, but it is not likely to remain stable for long given the processes of continued testing and refutation. And on Kuhn's views there is no one foundational 'pyramid' at all, but rather (in potential) a range of small ones, each of which may be built up and then degenerate again as puzzles turn into anomalies.

Needless to say there are shortcomings in both Popper's and Kuhn's views. One is that neither is a uniform description of the behaviour of research scientists. The Hungarian philosopher of science, Imre Lakatos, argued that whilst Kuhn's ideas were more characteristic of large-scale research programmes, Popper's were more applicable when such programmes were being worked out in detail. Another line of criticism has been that Popper goes too far in expecting all scientific theories to be falsifiable, whilst Kuhn does not go far enough in narrowing down what might pass as a valid paradigm.

The role of science as our most secure form of knowledge is not without its problems, therefore. In the next section we shall see further issues with the image of knowledge as resting on a commonly accepted body of evidence.

BEYOND REALISM

5.4 In the previous section we looked at two approaches that start from a presumption that scientific investigation can bring us objective knowledge of an external world. We saw that neither of these approaches eliminates an element of *inter-subjective* judgements of the scientific community.

In this section we will look at a cluster of critiques of the optimism that philosophers of science such as Popper and Kuhn have in scientific method as a source of knowledge. Some of these criticisms are especially acute in the area of social science.

The first of these issues springs from the work of Kuhn himself, and takes us back to *relativism* – the claim that knowledge is not absolute. Although Kuhn claimed not to be a relativist, his view of the incommensurability of paradigms can lend itself to relativist arguments. So if a particular theoretical framework is seen as a paradigm, then it would on this view not be open to critical scrutiny from outside. Much rests on exactly what counts as a paradigm in this argument. Kuhn seemed to think of these as wide ranging models, almost like foundation stones on which further research builds by elaborating the detail of how the paradigm applies in specific situations. Now, there is no specific reason why his analysis should only apply to concepts such as Darwinism or relativity. But it is incumbent on someone who uses a Kuhnian type argument to explain why a particular concept should be considered as paradigmatic – particularly in virtue of the idea that it cannot then be critiqued from the 'outside' as it were.

The list in Box 5.4 is a speculative suggestion as to what might count as a paradigm in management studies. Note that these form in effect an historical track of how management thought developed in the first seven decades of the twentieth century. So, 'scientific' management was *superseded* rather than directly refuted by human relations, without any specific event or discovery overcoming the general approach (even though research programmes such as the Hawthorne studies undermined its aspirations[7]). Another curious point is that in the last two decades or so, no overarching theoretical framework has sprung up to replace contingency

---

[7]The interested reader wishing to know more about the Hawthorne Studies is directed to Richard Gillespie's discussion *Manufacturing Knowledge: A History of the Hawthorne Experiments* (1991, Cambridge University Press).

or excellence – there have indeed been some important developments in the theory of organisations and management, but without the requisite level of generality.

BOX 5.4

'PARADIGMS' IN MANAGEMENT THOUGHT?

Following a Kuhnian approach to knowledge, we might ask ourselves whether any of the following might be considered as paradigms, in his strong sense of being resistant to critique from the 'outside':

scientific management: the idea prevalent in the early twentieth century that the job of management research was to use the methods of natural science to identify and analyse the processes whereby business activities could be most efficient

human relations: the view that as organisations were composed of human beings, the emphasis on processes was misplaced, and more important were the needs of individuals

socio-technical systems: this approach attempted to integrate both the focus on processes and the needs of individuals, postulating that the effectiveness of an organisation was a combination of the two variables

contingency theory: this was the idea that there is no single 'best' way to approach management, but that the effective organisation combines an approach that balances up a range of factors, to achieve a 'best fit' rather than a 'best of all' approach.

There are other wide scale approaches to management, such as the 'excellence' studies, but these are more clearly open-ended and open to criticism from external perspectives. The point about the list above is that each of the above could be regarded as self-contained.

A second issue relates to the language in which social phenomena are expressed, and the implications of this for what counts as knowledge. The language by which we refer to what is observable is not independent of what we believe or value. Even at the level of experiments that are measured by digital instruments there are assumptions built into the language in which we describe events: one set of flickers in the data is dismissed as 'noise' whilst another is seen as signifying a detectable pattern.

With social phenomena it becomes substantially more difficult to identify an objective descriptive language to identify events. Even as basic an idea as someone's preferences for washing powder over another cannot be unequivocally measured – asking someone is not necessarily robust, since that person may be influenced by many factors, such as the context of the request, whilst observing them may capture physical movements but not necessarily the intention behind these: someone buys one particular brand in a store, but there may be many reasons for this. Even in taking a physical movement as being a particular action we make assumptions about someone's intentions, for example.

There is a further twist to this question of the underlying assumptions of the language of social science, however. This is the controversial issue of the *ideological* dimension of the assumptions that are made by social scientists. On this argument, to conduct a research study – say an investigation into the ways senior executives manage performance – is to bring in certain values and beliefs: in this example, perhaps the idea that performance is something that needs to be managed by an external authority, or even more fundamentally that the organisation operates as a hierarchy with managers directing the levels of performance from 'above'.

This is complicated by the fact that as humans we are conscious of the ideas that others use to explain our behaviour, and hence can choose to act in conformance with or in contravention of such ideas. And further still our awareness of this language – and its many expressions in media, training courses, consultancy reports and the like – means that we are subject to the influence of those implicit assumptions made by those who issue such expressions. 'Strategy' suffers especially from this, as it has lost its original (and metaphorical) sense drawn from military theory, and seems nowadays to mean little more than any large-scale plan – with the assumption that such planning is always essential for success. In contrast the other key term used in military analysis – tactics – is hardly mentioned in management theory, downplayed as indicating a lower level both of activity and of thought, whilst in military operations it is often the core of a successful action or even of a whole campaign.

This gives rise to ideology, because many of the most fundamental assumptions regarding management and organisations are also related to overall theories of society, and often implicitly reflect *pro-business* stances. This is not surprising given that most management studies literature is intended to help organisations be more efficient and/or effective. But it can mean that the deepest criticisms of business and management (for example over its impact on the environment, treatment of workers' rights, creation of a consumerist culture etc.) are stifled and do not find their proper expression in mainstream management research.

One of the central examples of this tendency is an implicit approval, that some see in business management, for the idea of science and technology as a mechanism for continued social progress – this is often explicitly identified as the *modernist* trend in social thought. In contrast, *post-modernism* questions this, not only in respect of advanced market economies but also in relation to general global development. Michel Foucault, often associated with postmodernism (though he explicitly rejected this label himself), talked of the manner in which explanations of individual human thought and behaviour took on a form in each historical era that reflected the power relationships pertaining at that time. So during the during the sixteenth to eighteenth centuries, European politics and power relationships were dominated by the Reformation and the consequent loss of absolute power that the Roman Catholic church had held over ideas and learning: as a result there was a great emphasis on discovery, individual thought, and experimentation to test established ideas. In contrast the twentieth century was dominated by the rise of the major corporations, and hence much thought is correspondingly focused on large-scale business-friendly areas such as the role of 'big science' in technology. For Foucault power really *is* knowledge, not just in the sense that to know some fact is to enable one to act in relation to it, but also in the deeper sense that the kind of material that is accepted in a society as knowledge, at any one time, reflects and embodies the power relationships of that society – if something does not fit the spaces that the existing power situation creates for it, then it is not allowed to exist, there is no environment within which it may be considered.

This seems to suggest that thought is trapped by power – that our thinking only ever reflects the social structures in which we can operate intellectually, though it is not clear whether Foucault ever explicitly held this. In contrast Jurgen Habermas[8] felt that knowledge can transcend its social context. He developed a threefold categorisation of knowledge as incorporating *technical* elements as identified by natural science, *practical* ones that are reflected in social science and the humanities, and *emancipatory* elements which spring from his own idea of *critical theory*. This latter is the study of the underlying assumptions and structures within which our thinking takes place, and for Habermas was the key way in which we free ourselves from the domination of ideological assumptions built into the language we commonly use.

The key lesson to be learnt from these objections is that they undermine the idea that the study of management can use scientific methods to bring us knowledge. However, whilst it is clear that there are difficulties with saying the scientific approach is a consistently reliable source of knowledge, these arguments do not suggest that it is not a source of knowledge at all. Indeed, in many cases they presuppose that some validity is there in social science, just not one that we can rely on in all cases.

---

[8]Like Foucault, with whom he had a well documented but ultimately very respectful debate over some years, Habermas rejected postmodernism, even when agreeing with many ideas often associated with that term.

CONCLUSION

In this chapter we have looked at the scientific investigation as a basis for knowledge about organisations. The discussion has focused on natural science as a model for organisational knowledge, though we have seen that this does not account well for the investigation into social phenomena, where even the most basic descriptions contain substantial assumptions about society.

In the next chapter we will look at two key contextual aspects of knowledge.

QUESTIONS FOR CONSOLIDATION

1   How might you use the distinction between knowing how and knowing that when analysing the knowledge of a retail salesperson?

2   What are the primary differences between Kuhn's and Popper's theories of knowledge in science?

3   If asked to give an explanation of what a *brand* is, how do you think the accounts of the positivist and the postmodernist might differ? Would there be any aspects that might be in common between their views?

FURTHER READING

Archer, M., Bhaskar, R., Collier, A., Lawson, T. and Norrie, A. (1998) *Critical Realism: Essential Readings*. Routledge.

Feyerabend, P. (2010) *Against Method*, 4th edn. Verso Press.

Habermas, J. (1971) *Knowledge and Human Interests*. Heinemann.

Kuhn, T. (1996) *The Structure of Scientific Revolutions*, revised edn. University of Chicago Press.

Lakatos, I. and Musgrave, A. (eds) (1970) *Criticism and the Growth of Knowledge*. Cambridge University Press.

Popper, K. (2002) *The Logic of Scientific Discovery*, revised edn, Routledge.

Rabinow, P. ed. (1991) *The Foucault Reader*. Penguin.

CONTEXTS OF KNOWLEDGE IN ORGANISATIONS

After reading this chapter you should be able to:

- Analyse aspects of the media in which management knowledge is expressed
- Assess the respective merits of alternative approaches to knowledge in organisations based on non-western cultural foundations.

In Chapter 5 we looked at issues surrounding the view that the methods of science provide a basis for organisational knowledge. In this more practically focused chapter we move to some contextual features of knowledge in management.

Two contextual issues will be considered: firstly, how knowledge about management and organisations is presented to us, and secondly, how alternatives to western thinking relate to modernism.

THE IDEA OF 'SOCIAL' KNOWLEDGE

6.1 Knowledge is a collective asset of an organisation, *'I know that p'* implies that *'we know that p'* (the knowledge is there for use within the organisation). 'I believe that p' cannot be similarly generalised – belief does not have a stake in reality in the same way. We could put this by saying that believing something or not believing something are parallel, but if I know something, in some sense *I possess some connection with it*, which I lack if I do not know it.

Because of this, knowledge in an organisation is *collectable*, in a way that beliefs are not. The total knowledge of an organisation is the sum of all those individual connections with reality, each one being a separate asset. Whilst we can talk about the totality of beliefs in an organisation there is an important difference, as illustrated in Box 6.1 following.

BOX 6.1

KNOWING AND BELIEVING IN AN ORGANISATION

Savant Ltd has three members – person A, person B and person C.

A knows that p1, but does not know that p2 or p3
B knows that p2, but does not know that p1 or p3
C knows that p3, but does not know that p1 or p2

How much knowledge does Savant have? Three items, p1, p2 and p3, even though no one individual has access to more than one of these.

Credo Ltd also has three members, person Alpha, person Beta and person Gamma.

Alpha believes that p1 but does not believe that p2 or p3

Beta believes that p2 but does not believe that p1 or p3

Gamma believes that p3 but does not believe that p1 or p2

How many beliefs does Credo have? This question seems odd even to put – in one sense all of p1–3, in another none of them.

Believing something is thus not an asset in the way that knowing something can be.

However, common uses of 'know' do not always reflect this connection. We might attribute to a successful financial trader a 'knowledge' of the market, but their success might be just a good hit rate – statistically based decisions which work more often than not. While such individuals have *some* knowledge – for example the statistical models they are using, it is not clear that they *know* the market. If they gained a profit 95 percent of the time, one might be tempted to say that their understanding went beyond simply well evidenced beliefs. But if their success rate was down at 55 percent, it is less plausible to call this an intimate connection with reality, even though in the long run they will be successful. In ordinary discourse, however, people still call this a kind of knowledge, so we give this a different name – *social knowledge*.

What, then, do we mean by the idea of *social knowledge*? The sense considered here is related to Bakhtin's idea of *knowledge as constructed between individuals*.[1] Whilst this does not reject the idea of truth as being central to the nature of knowledge, it shifts focus from the attempt to uncover a sure basis for knowledge, towards a more coherentist approach where knowledge is to be understood in terms of its embeddedness in communicative networks.

---

[1]The next two paragraphs are not intended as an exegesis of Bakhtin's own thought.

This sense of social knowledge depicts the phenomenon as built up out of dialogue and agreement between individuals. Whilst it might be taken to imply that we *make* knowledge in our communities (which raises the issues of relativism discussed earlier in relation to Kuhn's view of science) this is not a necessary consequence. 'Social knowledge', on this interpretation, is more than simply widely held beliefs. It includes some deeper sense of how we build our understanding collectively. This echoes points relating to coherentism generally – if some item of thought fits into a certain network, that does not automatically make it knowledge. There is a spectrum: some items can only be made coherent by means of a number of additional assumptions and re-interpretations of existing ideas, whilst others may fit naturally and without any need for much revision of the network into which they are placed. In the case of social knowledge, we might add that there needs to be some process of dialogue between individuals to establish the common meanings and agreed elements, if something is to be part of such a socially defined network of knowledge.

Whilst the analysis in Box 6.2 seems plausible with respect to skills – *knowing how* – it is less clear whether the analysis could be extended to *knowing that*. The example of Savant Ltd does claim that we can say that in a case where each of three distinct individuals knows only p1, p2 and p3 respectively, the organisation as a whole can use all three as assets. But if p1–3 are the sole components of a further item of knowledge q1, we cannot automatically conclude that the organisation also knows that q1. 'To know' is *referentially opaque*, in the sense that we saw in an earlier chapter – I may know of financial formulae p1, p2 and p3, but unless I find out or am told that these collectively have the same effect as q1, I cannot be said to know this as well.

BOX 6.2

A POSSIBLE EXAMPLE OF SOCIAL KNOWLEDGE

Consider the idea of a *core competence*. In the so-called Resource Based View (commonly referred to simply as RBV) of strategic management,[2] a core competence is the capacity of an organisation to do something that provides a degree of uniqueness in the services offered by the firm in question. Interestingly, this makes use of a term – competence – that would

(Continued)

[2]The interested reader wishing to know more about the RBV is referred to 'Dynamic Capabilities and Strategic Management', by D. Teece, G. Pisano, and A. Shuen, in *Strategic Management Journal*, 18 (7): 509–533.

(Continued)

normally be used to refer to skills. But this is coupled with the fact that the 'skill' is attributed, not to individuals, but to the organisation as a whole.

There are identification issues here. Could a core competence be *only* attributable to a firm in its entirety? Can an organisation have a competence without any individual possessing it? Potentially, if that competence is analysable into a series of component parts, then it seems conceivable that a series of individuals might each know one of those components, and the organisation happens to be arranged so that these co-ordinate effectively. So the organisation might have the competence without any one individual either having that competence him- or herself, or even understanding that the organisation has this competence – echoes of our discussion of what defines an organisation in Chapter 1. But note that sheer possession of each of the components of a competence by an organisation's members is not on its own sufficient to say there is an organisation-wide competence.

THE MEDIA OF MANAGEMENT KNOWLEDGE

6.2 The main question in this section is the practical one of how much confidence we can have in the purported knowledge presented to us.

Knowledge for professional development

Typical examples of professional development include:

- attendance at training courses
- personal research using professional or academic books and articles
- embarking on specific work based projects
- working with or as a mentor.

This list is not comprehensive, but it provides a flavour of the range of things that might be potential sources of knowledge. But exactly what do these activities actually do for someone's knowledge?

Consider professional literature. This often comprises updates on matters such as changes in the law or success stories of individuals, coupled with articles on areas such as new techniques and their potential impact on the profession.

One issue with professional literature is the process whereby content is selected for publication, and the intentions behind authorship and publication. A commercial journal decides what to publish on the commercial basis of whether a certain topic is of interest to readers. Thus the key question for publication is not: is this *true*? but rather: is this *interesting*? This does not imply that periodicals ignore the truth of the content they publish: for example, some articles may reflect up-to-date ideas that have passed through reviewed journals. But it does imply that the truth of what is published is not a criterion for inclusion.[3]

Consider another source of professional knowledge, training courses. Again if we track the process by which such courses are designed and commissioned, we find that they are not necessarily grounded in what is demonstrably true. Many training operations are justified in terms of meeting identified demand, which is as much defined by what people *think* is necessary as by what knowledge is *actually there*. A government department may require that all professionals performing a certain task should be trained in a particular skill, but government decisions are not always based on established knowledge, often being made to improve the electability of a political group. Similarly a senior manager of a company may perceive a certain need, and request training providers develop courses to meet this. But consider the source of this perception – professional literature is subject to the issues already identified; if from another training course then the question arises as to the source of the content of this. As with publications, a training company might run a course because they see it as profitable – rather than having verified the truth of what is being presented.

It is important to recognise that this is not a practical argument to suggest that all such learning is valueless, or that publishers and trainers have no scruples as to what they publish or deliver. Rather it is the *philosophical* argument that these cannot be completely *relied upon* to give us knowledge in the strong senses which we have been discussing in the last two chapters. There is room for doubt here, that is the point.

Academic publications

Even within the supposed bastions of knowledge – academic publications – there are potential question marks over reliability. At the level of academic publication, all knowledge is still work-in-progress, as Popper noted. The most up-to-date work is the most provisional, and only after a period of time is it absorbed into the general consensus.

Academic journals generally work by a process of content being reviewed by expert peers, who agree that a paper of good quality may be published, or they may require revisions, or reject it because it is not sound. Many

---

[3]One should add that particular facts are generally checked out for their truth in such magazines - e.g. whether or not a particular government department has exceeded its budget by 25 percent. But arguably these are checked not for the sake of truth but for the sake of litigation avoidance.

papers move successfully through this process because they fit specific *formal* expectations of journal reviewers and editors, general academic grounds such as: is the argument sound? do the research methods follow the expected norms in the discipline? does the paper say something original, or is it an important test of other people's work? Furthermore, some academic work is of the form of a try-out: the author is saying – here is a *possibility*, as an invitation for others to test this in different contexts, for repeatability, or perhaps for coherence with other work. So the fact of publication is not a guarantee of truth. In general papers are published on the basis of *credibility* rather than validity. In all academic disciplines credible papers are often published that after a period of investigation are rejected by the community of scholars; this is how academic progress works.

There are further distortions of the academic publishing process that undermine its claims to be a uniformly reliable channel for the dissemination of established truths. Academic practitioners – professors, lecturers, research fellows – are expected as part of their jobs to publish papers, and their research performance is measured in many countries on this basis. Hence a researcher is under pressure to submit papers for publication at the earliest opportunity, giving rise to the temptation to present incomplete data as a coherent result, to ignore or suppress countervailing data. Again, this is not an attempt to argue that academics or journal publishers are charlatans, but simply to point out shortcomings to our confidence in academic material as knowledge.

The location and storage of knowledge

A closely related question is the issue of how knowledge is captured and held available for access by others. In short – exactly *where* is knowledge? The sources we have discussed with regard to dissemination are in the main also the locales for knowledge – texts, digital sources, experts, and sometimes the 'ordinary' person in the street.

However, these locations can be inadequate for a manager to access the knowledge they need. Suppose I want to set up a new production system in my factory, based on something that I have read about, involving the idea of a production circle.[4] At this stage the only knowledge I have is what I have gained from my reading. I now locate more extensive literature about the concept, and invite a production circle consultant to carry out a feasibility study of how the idea might work in my factory. In addition, to help me implement this, I visit other factories where the concept has been applied with success.

We have already seen that with the best will in the world textual knowledge is not on its own a sure foundation for our knowledge. Still less is

---

[4]At the time of writing this is a fictitious idea to illustrate the argument.

electronically presented information, where the culture of open access and contribution means that a large amount of content is potentially unverified.[5]

What of field researches? Presumably, unless the consultant is a fraud, the report that they write is directly based on data they have collected and analysed. Being so, it will doubtless suffer from the 'standard' shortcomings that all social research risks encountering, amongst these being: potential researcher bias in data collection; sampling bias; the wrong questions being asked; respondents distorting their responses in relation to what they think are the intentions of the researcher. Similar issues will arise when I speak to other managers who have successfully implemented the concept.

The trend to publish success

There is yet a further issue: successes with managerial innovations are frequently written about and reported in the literature. Fewer are the reports of failures – a major disaster is newsworthy and will be reported, but an unexciting failure is not interesting and therefore not likely to be disseminated widely.[6] This therefore distorts the overall picture of what I am trying to find out: I am likely to access copious data about successful examples of implementation, but far less when it has not gone well. So I assume that usually this is a success, when actually the concept may at least as often have failed. There is a similar issue with consultancy, that material which conflicts with the overall conclusion of the research is underplayed. This is a consequence of how ideas are communicated in business, as in academia: a clear message, simply and directly expressed, is one that is easily understood; a messy or ambiguous message is often ignored, perhaps because it needs to be carefully considered over time, when managers do not have this luxury. It is more effective to state simply 'x', rather than 'x except in situations a or b, when y needs to be combined with x or z'. Complex messages are problematic to understand, so the person creating the content will try to find ways to present the material in a clear, simple and summarised fashion.[7]

But even when all this goes well, there is still a gap between what I have collected and what I need to know. Organisations are complex clusters of human beings (themselves very complex things) co-ordinating in intricate ways, in a constantly shifting environment. However good the comparisons

---

[5] Open access and contribution does not *necessarily* mean that content is unverified – some 'wiki' style online sources include review as part of their processing. Whilst this suffers from the same shortcomings as was discussed in relation to academic journals, it remains superior to unverified material.

[6] This is less true with academic publishing where there is occasionally published research reporting incomplete or even failed initiatives.

[7] Again it should be stressed that this paragraph, like earlier discussions, is not a charge of dishonesty but an indication of potential weakness.

with other companies, each application of a concept to a new organisation is a novel and creative act. No two organisations are ever sufficiently similar for the implementation of an idea to be any more than a guide to implementation in the other. Hence the key question to which I as the manager require an answer – *will the concept work in my factory?* – is unanswerable, as far as drawing on previous knowledge is concerned. I have to generate my own knowledge in order to implement the concept. This implies that, in principle, **generalised results have only limited value in terms of management knowledge.** Organisations are too different in their detail for broad patterns to be much help in deciding what to do. More important are concrete, particular, local solutions to problems, which by their nature only afford limited comparison with other contexts.

Knowledge and utility

Our discussion of the media of knowledge in management has come to a sceptical conclusion. For it indicates that the search for scientifically based generalisable knowledge is, if not impossible, at least not efficient, in comparison with the concrete knowledge embodied in the design of localised solutions.

This does not imply, however, that we should abandon the search for generalisable knowledge entirely in favour of more narrowly based, situation-specific knowledge. Rather it indicates that we reframe our understanding of what knowledge does for management.

We can think of knowledge about organisations and management as located along a spectrum relating to their direct relationship with managerial practice, as Box 6.3 illustrates.

BOX 6.3

THE CONTINUUM OF MANAGERIAL IDEAS

pure scientific universals – true in all cases; precisely defined criteria for application that may exclude many practical contexts

'applied' scientific results – not universally true but apply in most cases within a defined range

reflective observations of individual practitioners – true for most experiences of the individual concerned

specific practical solutions to particular problems – true in one individual case

anecdotes – refer directly to specific cases but without any precisely defined criteria.

The degree of control and structure in management 'knowledge' varies inversely with its ease of application – the rough and highly individualised anecdote refers to a specific situation, but says little or nothing about other cases, whilst the well evidenced and well structured and tested result applies to all cases but only within carefully and often narrowly defined criteria. Further, when we say that something is true, this implies that for all the different ways in which the statement might be tested, the same result will be achieved. This is clear for the pure scientific statement. But as we move away from a precise structure it becomes less certain. At the far end of the spectrum, an anecdote may reflect maybe just one way in which a phenomenon is presented to us, so that it reflects a particular observation and no more.

In this section we have looked at knowledge about management, construed in its 'social' sense, as this manifests itself in concrete channels of dissemination. Contextual aspects undermine the aspiration that we can be assured of accessing truth via these channels. Furthermore, the more universal an idea is the less directly does it apply in concrete management contexts.

Having discussed at some length these shortcomings of the idea of knowledge in management, we will move in the next section to looking at knowledge as it is manifest in other contexts than the western modernist or 'scientific' context.

NON-WESTERN PERSPECTIVES ON KNOWLEDGE IN ORGANISATIONS

6.3 In the previous sections we have been looking at contextual issues relating to the form in which knowledge might be said to be available to organisations. In this section we shall consider a different kind of context – that of the culture in which knowledge appears and is presented. We will look at several alternative belief-systems to see what they say about organisations and management.[8] But first consider again western modernity.

Modernity

The 'western' conception of science and knowledge can be regarded as *progressively foundationalist*, depicting our knowledge of organisations as growing in volume and depth, as ever more research is successfully completed. On this view, as knowledge grows so management actions can become more accurately targeted and based on objective insights instead of anecdotalism. This confidence in the progressive nature of research as leading to continual improvements in techniques and practice is central to

[8]But we will only scratch the surface of this range. The reader is referred to Worsley (1997) for more detail.

what is often called *modernity*. This term has acquired various interpretations, but it is generally agreed that the 'modern' age began in the seventeenth century, with the release of European cultures from the influence of the Christian church, which had previously dominated the development of knowledge. Tradition was replaced by scientific method, as a kind of mechanics of objectivity. Modernity carries the optimism that science would gradually erode all human problems, as objective knowledge is discovered and used as the basis for more effective practices.

It is questionable whether this is exclusively a 'western' conception. Scientific methods of investigation were in use in China several centuries before they were common in Europe, so that by the year 1200 CE that country had already made their 'four great inventions' (gunpowder, paper, printing and the magnetic compass). The emphasis on experience and investigation as key elements of knowledge was also important in the distinction drawn between thought and verification by the medieval thinker Ibn-Sina.[9]

Nevertheless, the great leap forward provided by the industrial revolution was fuelled in part by the modernist approach, and given that this took place mainly in Europe we shall continue with the association between modernity and 'western' thinking, even if this is an oversimplification.

Spiritual-religious world-views and organisational knowledge

Under this heading could be included a variety of 'non-western' philosophies, such as Confucianism, Buddhism, Islam. As noted above, although in the modern era Islam is often seen as 'non-western' this was not the case in the time of thinkers such as Ibn-Sina or Ibn-Rushd, who developed some of the ideas of Greek philosophy, passing these on in turn to Christian philosophers such as Aquinas. Also one must clarify that not all these traditions are deistic in the western sense. For example, although Confucius believed in a deity, his work was less religious than spiritual. Nevertheless these approaches share the similarity that they relate knowledge to a spiritual conception of the individual human being, and acknowledge an ethical dimension to this.

The main contributions of Confucius are to be found in relation to ethics and political philosophy. He wrote widely on ethics and government, and has been compared to several thinkers in the West in relation to some of his ideas, such as the importance of virtue and moderation[10] and the Golden

---

[9]Known in Europe as Avicenna. Arguably, he could be counted as part of the European tradition since he was one of the key Islamic philosophers who preserved and extended the work of Aristotle in the so-called 'dark' ages, being a significant influence, along with Ibn-Rushd (Averroes), on St Thomas Aquinas.

[10]As Aristotle argued two centuries later.

Rule – that we should treat other people the same way as we would wish to be treated ourselves.

However, there are some important insights that he has in relation to leadership and learning. His view of education was deliberately integrative – his dictum 'he who learns but does not think is lost; he who thinks but does not learn is in great danger'[11] exhorts the individual to maintain a balance between knowledge and reflection. The emphasis on reflection can be seen elsewhere – 'The man with humanity speaks with hesitation ... Since to do something is difficult, can one speak about it without hesitation?'[12] Whilst the main intention of this characteristically taciturn statement relates to prudence, there is also the hint of a specific approach to action. Elsewhere Confucius develops this situational approach, arguing that context determines when it is appropriate to act or think first. Hierarchy was an important related notion for Confucius, who argued that the success of the leadership role is in part down to the behaviour of followers as well as leaders – both have their duties: humans have an interconnectedness, and each person thus needs to strive to fit their role.

One influential implication of this has been the focus on relationships in public life in China – a phenomenon known as *guanxi*, which loosely translates as relationship, connection or even rapport. This takes the idea of human interconnectedness as implying that for business to be successful, there needs to be a strong *guanxi* between members. This has had a significant impact on Chinese business practices – for example, recruitment of new staff is often focused on people who already have a family or friendship connection with a firm. In many countries this might be seen as nepotism, but the rationale in the Chinese context is that the large-scale commitment to employing someone is more effective the better one knows that person.

In general the philosophical vision of Confucius is centred on humanity and on the duties and responsibilities of leaders. There is less directly on the nature of knowledge, but implicitly this focus almost makes a statement by default – that the conception of applying an objective body of knowledge to an independent and inert phenomenon such as an institution or organisation (or in his terms, the government or empire) is misplaced.

Buddhism is more explicitly a religion with implications for knowledge, although here the idea of a 'religion' is not synonymous with following a deity. The key features of Buddhism are, arguably, (a) reality is in a constant state of dynamic change; (b) all phenomena are interlinked in a network of causes and effects; (c) beings such as humans follow a cycle of birth, death and rebirth in different forms depending on one's conduct; (d) this cycle of reincarnation is linked to our enslavement to desire, and maintains beings in a condition of unhappiness; (e) it is possible to break out of this, by

---

[11]Confucius, *Analects*, 2.15.

[12]*Analects*, 12.3.

recognising the transience of reality and adopting practices such as meditation to eliminate the dependence on desire or pleasure.

The idea that all things are continually in flux was also used by some Buddhists to argue that even metaphysical concepts such as being and non-being are meaningless, and that all phenomena should be treated as provisional or transient. Arguably this could be the basis for a conception of organisation as a temporary configuration of people, resources and intentions.

In contrast with Confucius, the Buddha focused on individual perfection, rather than the interaction between humans. The emphasis on individual enlightenment does not say much *directly* about organised human behaviour. However, the inter-relationship between all things does have implications for how people interact. One aspect is that decision making, whilst not so overtly consensus oriented as the Confucian ideal, should still aim for harmony. A second aspect of this is that for Buddhists all nature is of equal ethical value – plants, insects, as much as humans. Hence the western conception of nature as an inert object to be exploited or controlled is misplaced here. This has important implications for the Buddhist attitude to the environment and conservation – and hence for the role of organisations in this process.

The idea that desire is something that has to be transcended, and that it binds us to a lower condition of life, has other implications for the western market society, in which the possession of objects has acquired an almost symbolic value. In contrast the Buddhist ideal is for restraint – not deliberate hardship, but the freedom from desire. This does not directly imply that possessions or wealth are wrong, but it does undermine the main reason why someone would want these.

Overall Buddhism's most striking contributions to the understanding of organisations are the emphasis on harmony and continuity, the focus on collaborative decision making, and the implied critique of consumption, as illustrated above.

These two spirituo-religious philosophies, although different in their fundamental tenets, have similarities so far as their implications for organisations are concerned. Both hold a form of ethic based on moderation, both promote the idea of humans living in harmony with nature, both encourage collaboration rather than conflict, and both lay an emphasis on reflection as a key element in human growth. It is also true that these say relatively little about the idea of organisational knowledge as such, although their views of the role of humans in nature carry some implications for the idea of science as an independent form of enquiry.[13]

---

[13]Note that these are two specific examples, and in those regions where these philosophies have adherents there are many other philosophical positions, theorists and debates.

Traditional philosophical views and organisational knowledge

We will turn now to examples of philosophical views that have a less precise origin. It is tempting to call these 'folk' philosophies, if that term did not suggest that they are less worthy of serious consideration. We will call them 'traditional' views, meaning that they have evolved over long periods. We will look specifically at two examples of these, the African concept of *Ubuntu*, and the Australian one of the *Dreamtime*, though other approaches, such as the metaphysical views of native North Americans, would also merit consideration in depth.

Ubuntu may be encountered in different interpretations in different parts of central and southern Africa. It is thus less a culture-specific concept than a *regional* one, much as some of the great religions cross national and ethnic boundaries. Though of some antiquity, the idea of Ubuntu has been refreshed over the last few decades.

Ubuntu can be summarised as the idea that all human beings are interconnected. One slogan associated with Ubuntu is the saying 'I am what I am because of who we all are.'[14] This has been applied in many contexts, for example as the basis for equality of opportunity; the right for participation among all human beings; the justification for practising generosity towards those less fortunate than ourselves; the conception of crime as a defect of a *community* rather than an act of deviance; and the basis for the idea that a leader is not 'above' their subjects but is more like a 'first among equals' and only leads by virtue of the will of those who are led. Ubuntu has also become enshrined in some of the constitutional systems of southern Africa – for example being one of the five key principles of Botswana and having been used in some policy documents in South Africa.

A number of key implications for organisations can be identified from the underlying conception of Ubuntu. First, human interconnectedness suggests, not just the importance of individuals in a firm working closely together, but also, that the work of the firm needs to be connected with that of others. One interpretation of this is to critique possessive individualism as the basis for market economies, and to reject competition as a fundamental driver of business.

A second implication is the idea of leadership without superiority. According to Ubuntu, leaders do have authority and they retain ascendancy, but this is based on the willing co-operation of those who are led. Someone who has to coerce those they lead is not an Ubuntu leader.

A related third point is the nature of decision making. Under Nelson Mandela the ruling party of South Africa, the African National Congress,

---

[14]It is no accident that a computer operating system built on open source principles borrowed the term as a title, for the developers of the Linux-based system explicitly quoted Ubuntu ideas such as working collaboratively with others to develop collective goals.

following Ubuntu principles, strove to achieve consensus in decisions. Voting was seen as in effect a failure of the decision-making process, in that it created winners but also losers, directly countering Ubuntu principles. The implication here is that a sound decision takes account of all viewpoints. There are corollaries to this: one needs to devote sufficient time to developing a solution acceptable to all, and there needs to be a definition of just who 'we' are. But overall this aspect of Ubuntu suggests collaborative, team oriented values and decisions. It is worth noting, however, the potential negative consequence that consensual decision making can sometimes degenerate into conformism.

Ubuntu, therefore, is a well established principle of humanity, which has been elaborated in various ways in relation to organisations. Overall it is in line with western consensus based organisation theory as developed over the last two decades, but it goes further than simply a theory of the firm, and suggests that the global economy as a whole can be regarded as an interconnected community.

Like Ubuntu, the Australian concept of the Dreamtime is a continent-wide phenomenon. This is a mythical-metaphysical account of the origin of the world. When the material world came into being, a number of pre-existing souls decided to enter all the animals, including one that became human. Native Australians believe that as these newly-'souled' creatures travelled the continent, they left *imprints* on the land. The stories of their travels and those imprints are summed up in a collection of narratives they call the *songlines*. Due to the imprinting mentioned above these narratives also reflect the geographical structure of the continent – for example a winding river might have been 'created' by a twisting snake. A song therefore might relate something about a snake twisting, interpretable by one who understands the songs as indicating the geophysical feature in question. Tribes maintained these songlines through local tribal learning, song, dance, visual art and other cultural forms. Many of these songlines enabled indigenous Australians to travel across vast distances, always finding shelter, food and water in what is not generally a very fertile continent. These narratives do not form a single consistent whole, but more a series of connected networks of stories – there are significant variations across the continent, but they share a similar structure.

As with the other non-western views considered, the natural world is given far greater significance in comparison with western modernity, and again we encounter the idea of humans needing to live in harmony with nature. Unlike these other views, however, there has been no association of Dreamtime with industrial activity. Nevertheless, the survival of the songline traditions over thousands of years and thousands of miles testifies to a degree of inter-tribal collaboration, in contrast to the competitive approach to relationships that characterises western market economies, and the value of preserving knowledge over long periods of time, in contrast with the short-term focus characteristic of western business.

Overall, what do we learn from these examples of non-western belief systems, in respect of organisations? First, the perception of nature as being something to *accommodate* rather than master, implying that the exploitation of natural resources needs to be balanced against sustainability. Second, the focus on consensual relationships rather than conflictual ones. And underlying these issues is the sense of a fundamental interlinkage of ethical and natural issues.

Although there is little that is directly related to management knowledge, these belief systems help us identify assumptions made by the western modernistic approach to organisations. One is the view of the natural world as explicable without any assumption of an underlying intelligence, and thus without us having an ethical duty towards 'Nature' (apart from certain sentient animals). Hence the main interest that humans have in it is to generate the necessities for life. Scientific investigation of the natural world, therefore, deals objectively with this neutral subject matter, to which humans can apply technology without needing to consider any outcomes except as they impinge on our own lifestyles.

A second assumption is that human possessiveness has no upper limit. This underpins the market orientation of modern economics where individuals compete in markets to generate an ever greater capacity to possess. A further corollary of this is that competition by definition creates winners and losers, hence human life is necessarily unequal in terms of the benefits of collective activity. In contrast this is missing from all the non-western approaches that we considered.

A third assumption is that the basic social unit is the individual. Decisions and outcomes are conceived in terms of individual actors and impacts on individual stakeholders, thus underpinning ethical debates such as rights to property, or the allocation of the rewards of business.

How do these ideas relate back to the earlier discussions of knowledge? One feature is that the systematic approaches evidenced in discussions of natural science do not seem to be in evidence. There is an element of paradigm in a concept such the songlines, where an overarching idea is then worked out in detail for different 'lines' though the suggestion that such a framework might break down would appear to be misplaced. The idea of laying a foundation, or of identifying a bedrock that is the basis for our certainty, is absent. Indeed with Confucius there is no obvious unity to his ideas, rather a loose collection of thoughts that exemplify a range of themes. Perhaps the main lesson to be learned here is that the western idea that our knowledge has to be understood in structural terms is not shared in other contexts.

In this section we have looked at comparisons between the so-called 'western' *modernistic* approach to knowledge and organisations, and some world-views from other cultures. It is worth noting, as a final comment here, that the discussion above is not a description of how people actually feel or behave. Clearly, African leaders may behave in a way that violates the principles of Ubuntu, just as some entrepreneurs who profess to be Buddhist may not actually make efforts to control their own enslavement to desire, and Chinese manufacturers may not exhibit the virtues of the wise leader. This is not a refutation of the ideas we have been discussing, just as the fact that some western managers fail to exhibit charity in their business dealings is a refutation of Christianity. The importance of such ideas is less in their explicit manifestations than in the influence of the assumptions that they may, almost subliminally, bring to people's thinking.

In this chapter we have looked at two different contextual aspects of knowledge about management. First, how specific modes of dissemination affect the validity of organisational 'knowledge', and second, the implications of certain non-western belief systems. There is no single conclusion to be drawn from these, save that the idea that there is something 'special' about our *knowledge* of management that ties it more closely with the truth than a well-founded belief is not made any more clear from these considerations. Indeed, in the case of different cultural belief systems, evidence plays so different a role from that of western science that it undermines further our confidence that the organisational world can be investigated objectively.

QUESTIONS FOR CONSOLIDATION

1   What are the key questions that would need to be addressed when evaluating a management consultant's report on an organisation?

2   How would you resolve the difference between two stakeholders with different cultural assumptions about how your firm should exploit the environment?

FURTHER READING

Bakhtin, M. M. (1984) *Problems of Dostoevsky's Poetics*, edited and translated by Caryl Emerson. University of Minnesota Press.

Lutz, David (2009) 'African Ubuntu Philosophy and Global Management', *Journal of Business Ethics*, 84: 313–28.

Roberts, R. and Jay Wood, W. (2010) *Intellectual Virtues: An Essay in Regulative Epistemology*. Oxford University Press.

Worsley, P. (1997) *Knowledges*. Profile Books.

POSTSCRIPT TO SECTION 2

In these past three chapters we have taken traditional issues relating to knowledge and expanded them in the context of management and organisations. Some of the lessons we can draw from these discussions are as follows:

- Knowledge should in some way have a more intimate relationship with the truth than just belief, and in some way we expect to be able to experience this.
- We cannot be absolutely certain about very much at all in the external perceivable world, but this lack of complete certainty does not necessitate the acceptance of scepticism.
- The idea that knowledge is justified true belief is insufficient, on its own, as a complete definition of knowledge.
- When we try to structure or systematise our knowledge, there are two overarching approaches that tend to be used – one emphasises the coherence between the whole network of things we know, and the other stresses the way in which knowledge has a foundation in those items of which we feel more certain.
- Our confidence in science as a source of knowledge is in the main based on its ability to self-critique and move forward, rejecting incorrect ideas as evidence continues to build up.
- Alternative views of the progress of scientific knowledge focus on the openness of scientific theories to the possibility of refutation, or on the manner in which a dominant idea or paradigm gradually declines in value to eventually be replaced.
- The media via which knowledge about organisations is expressed and disseminated all have various potential flaws which can undermine the validity of what is presented.
- The 'western modernistic' perspective tends to treat the natural world as an independent entity that can be investigated objectively; belief systems originating in non-western cultures do not share this assumption, are less structural in approach, and tend to be more inclusive in their conception of collaborative decision making.

It is appropriate to relate these conclusions more directly to management practice, and this concluding section looks at Knowledge Management (henceforth KM), currently one of the most prevalent management concepts, at least in terms of the frequency of its occurrence. Popularised[15] by the work of Nonaka and Takeuchi, it lays emphasis on the need of modern organisations to treat the knowledge available to them as a key strategic resource – one that when properly managed can provide a critical competitive advantage in a market environment.

KM has a range of different manifestations – an information systems aspect, a human learning aspect, an enterprise and innovation aspect, to name but three. All however share, amongst other things, certain assumptions:

- that knowledge – social knowledge in the sense we have discussed earlier – is a critical resource for an organisation
- that it may be analysed in relation to how clearly it is represented externally
- that it may be collected and in some way conserved to the benefit of an organisation.

Following the work of the philosopher Michael Polanyi, knowledge management (KM) theorists postulated that although sometimes we are consciously aware of what we know (explicit knowledge) there are also occasions when we are not so conscious (tacit knowledge).

Explicit knowledge – such as someone knowing full well that they can drive a tractor, or that they can speak both Cantonese and Mongolian languages fluently – may present practical problems if there is no one to whom the knowledge may be transferred, or if no one with similar skills may be found when the individual in question leaves. But it does not present the theoretical difficulties of tacit knowledge – what exactly is the knowledge in question, how we can make use of it and how we can sustain or conserve it.

A central task of many KM projects is thus often seen as ensuring that tacit knowledge is recognised and used effectively within an organisation. Some knowledge management writers talk of how it is *captured*, though this may be an overly ambitious aspiration, since a lot even of explicit knowledge is lost when people leave a company.

This distinction between the explicit and the tacit can become blurred once it is examined more closely.

Someone may know *something* but not be clear exactly about what it is. So there is a tacit as well as an explicit element to the same piece of knowledge here. Further an individual might have true belief about their knowledge (say, that there is some kind of skill involved in what he did) and also what may be a false belief as well (that everybody could do it). It would seem that

---

[15]But not originated.

'capturing' such an unclear piece of knowledge is not on its own likely to be that effective.

Some KM theorists have moved beyond the simple tacit/explicit distinction, and talk instead of the *degree of externalisation* of knowledge. In other words, knowledge needs to be communicable to others, via external manifestations – linguistically, or perhaps via diagrams, symbols, etc. In this form it may be 'captured' and then stored, for example in a database. Nonaka in particular talks of externalisation followed by re-internalisation.

Whilst being captured and stored may be *necessary* for knowledge to be managed, is this *sufficient*? Is everything that is subject to such processes knowledge, even in the social sense of knowledge?

Sometimes there may be organisational pressure on individuals to share their skills, so that others may benefit from the dissemination of knowledge. In this case there may be an effort to find some explicit formulation that is intended to capture knowledge. One way an organisation might 'capture' someone's unclarified and unconceptualised knowledge could be by discussing how that individual thinks about their work as they do it. There are various ways this might work – through cognitive mapping, or perhaps by an action learning set, where several people use non-directive dialogue techniques to help develop their knowledge. The optimistic view about what then happens is that over time and given the right process, the individual becomes able to express what they know and initially cannot articulate in a way that is comprehensible to others.

Now, is this the same thing that they knew before? One assumption of KM is that buried in the original behaviour is a kernel of knowledge that somehow gets transferred to its later context, where it is openly expressed in a structured format. However, this seems at least to require an explanation as to exactly what remains the same to be transferred between the unstructured knowledge and the explicit articulated version. It might be easier to say that the knowledge is not conserved but *transformed* by the process of dialogue into something that can be shared by others. On this interpretation knowledge management does not capture anything but *adapts* it.

The KM theorist might at this point ask whether it matters. From an organisation's point of view, we start with an individual who doesn't really understand how they can do something, and later on after some dialogue, we have several individuals who, helped by their discussion, can achieve the same outcome, even if they have done more than simply work out what is done. Maybe we can say this is less a case of *disseminating existing knowledge* and more a case of *collaborating in new knowledge* – a form of learning rather than of sharing, though this suggests that knowledge management is not much different from organisational learning in general.

A bigger problem, however, goes back to calling this knowledge at all. Most of the processes that KM theory discusses tend to be mechanisms for sharing statements, beliefs and practices – for example dialogue, communities of practice,[16] expert systems software. Whilst processes such as dialogue might have some verifying element, the simple inclusion of some element in an 'expert' system does not, on its own. And even with a self-critical, investigative community of practice, it is an article of *faith* that this will lead to the verification of an item as knowledge rather than simply as a useful belief.

Let us turn to a concept that can have a positive practical benefit in relation to this issue, but also represents a departure from traditional attempts to explain knowledge discussed in earlier chapters.

VIRTUE EPISTEMOLOGY

Until now we have been asking questions such as: what makes something knowledge? Can we sure about what is presented to us as knowledge? and so on. These all focus on *what is known*.

But knowledge is not independent of human beings. It only exists when people know it. So perhaps the orientation of epistemology is wrong when it looks at the *object* of knowledge; maybe instead we should interpret the question of what it is to know something as what kind of individual can be the *bearer* of knowledge.

The idea that there are features of human personality that are relevant to what and how we know things dates back at least as far as Aristotle, who talked about the 'intellectual' virtues (to distinguish them from the moral virtues which we will encounter in a later chapter): these are features of someone's character that are likely to lead to sound processes of knowledge acquisition. In the late twentieth century this idea became popular amongst philosophers as a potential way out of some key debates in epistemology, such as the conflict between foundationalism and coherentism.

Essentially the thesis of virtue epistemology (henceforth VE) is that knowledge is what results when people manifest the intellectual virtues.[17] This does not mean that acting in an intellectually virtuous manner automatically leads to knowledge. Rather it indicates that the adoption of the intellectual virtues is *a reliable means* of attaining knowledge. Repeated and careful action in line with these virtues can mean that we increase our chances of attaining the truth about a certain question, as these virtues will help us weed out unjustified beliefs in favour of those with an ever stronger justification.

What counts as an intellectual virtue? Two general camps identify them as, on the one hand intellectual *faculties*, such as perception and memory,

---

[16]A group of professionals with similar interests in an area of knowledge and practice, who meet physically or virtually from time to time to share and discuss techniques, ideas, materials, learning etc.

[17]There are several variants of VE currently, and the account given here is only one of several ways to elaborate the concept.

and on the other *character traits,* such as open-mindedness or conscientious-ness. Aristotle identified faculties such as theoretical wisdom, understanding, intelligence, which are clearly part of our mental apparatus, rather than of our personality – though this may determine how we use these faculties. Lists of character traits might include honesty, courage, open-mindedness, integrity, a love of truth or knowledge, humility and so on. Some items on such lists can cross over into what are also regarded as ethical virtues.

Virtue epistemology does not solve all the big problems of knowledge; it says very little about scepticism, for example. Also it remains unclear just how some particular traits are intimately linked with knowledge – or is it just that these happen to be statistically better at getting us to the truth than other means such as tossing coins?

Nevertheless, what is especially interesting about the contents of VE theories is the overlap with some aspects of Knowledge Management. In its more organisational interpretations, KM identifies elements such as an open culture, avoidance of blame, high levels of trust, readiness to chal-lenge orthodoxy and continuous learning. Whilst these terms are not state-ments of intellectual virtue, there are some clear parallels: open-mindedness and an open culture; the love of truth and continuous learning; intellectual courage and the challenge to orthodoxy.

It would be stretching the parallels to claim that knowledge management is best seen as an embodiment of virtue epistemology. Nevertheless it could be argued that in a collective, a way forward for the management of knowl-edge might be to focus in depth on what it means for an individual or a collective to be good at generating and using knowledge. And in the matter of using knowledge, we move to the next section of this book, that concerns itself with actions of individuals and organisations – how these take place and what they ought to aim for.

In this postscript to Section 2, we have considered knowledge as some-thing to be managed within organisations. Where Knowledge Management initiatives proceeded on a basis that knowledge can be identified and pro-cessed independent of how it is possessed by someone, it seemed to present similar problems to the traditional philosophical approaches. The parallels between this and virtue epistemology however – the latter being the focus on knowers rather than on what is known – are suggestive of a richer under-standing of what it is to know something collectively.

FURTHER READING

Fairweather, A. and Zagzebsky, L.,(eds) (2001) *Virtue Epistemology.* Oxford University Press.
Nonaka, I. and Tacheuchi, H. (1995) *The Knowledge Creating Company.* Oxford University Press.

WHAT TO DO? MAKING DECISIONS AND ACTING ETHICALLY IN MANAGEMENT

3

We finished Section 2 of this discussion with a series of unresolved questions about our level of confidence about what we know about management and organisations. The most obvious and important upshot of this is how this affects the decisions we make and our actions, and it is this to which we will turn in this final part.

There are two different aspects to the question of what to do. There is the fundamental question of what happens when I do something – how do thoughts, beliefs and motives turn into choices, and from there into action? And then there is the question of what choices should I make, on what bases and with what intentions and outcomes? We shall look at the first of these questions in Chapter 7, where themes from Section 2 of the book will recur. After that, we will turn in the final two chapters to the question of what choices should be made, individually in organisations and collectively.

In these chapters we will not aim at *normative* conclusions – suggestions as to what people actually ought to do. Rather the aim is to understand what is involved in such decisions, what do we actually mean by the idea of goodness and morality when considered in an organisational context, sometimes called *meta-ethics*. This does not mean that no normative statements will be encountered here but rather that the aim is to get behind what such statements involve – the idea of an action, the idea of individual morality, and what sense we can attach to the idea of a corporation's responsibility.

INDIVIDUAL AND ORGANISATIONAL ACTION

ACTION AND COLLECTIVES

7.1 Before we can consider what makes something a good action, we need to understand how action takes place at all. In this context of managerial action we need also to consider what it means to talk about a 'collective' action.

Enron is generally regarded as one of the worst corporate failures of modern times. Its CEO, Kenneth Lay, assisted by other company officials, over-reported its revenues and used a range of managerial techniques to conceal losses, so that external investors were misled into believing that it was successful. As losses mounted Lay and others sold their own shares in the company before the price collapsed – still encouraging other investors to hold on to their stock. Eventually the losses, and the fraud, became public knowledge. The share price fell to a fraction of its peak value, Lay and others were imprisoned, the company went bankrupt, employees lost their jobs but sometimes also pensions they had invested with the company, and their auditors, Arthur Anderson, shut down due to the poor publicity concerning their failure to report the fraud.

There are several unethical aspects here. But it is also a good example of part of the difficulty of identifying actions in a corporate environment. Two issues in particular can be considered – first, the relationships between intention, action and outcome, and second, the idea of a *corporate* action.

In its purest form, as depicted below, an action is an event knowingly set in motion by an individual, with the intention of achieving an outcome. Events in the external world always carry some degree of uncertainty, so there are almost always unforeseen outcomes: I rush to catch a ball and do not notice that I also tread on a caterpillar. So every action therefore takes some risks.

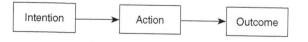

FIGURE 7.1

The phenomenon known as *moral luck* is often presented as a peripheral factor in the evaluation of action, whereas in fact it is a feature of all acts. Mostly luck falls in our favour – we behave in a way that we estimate will bring about a certain outcome, and it does. Moral luck is more noticeable when it does not go our way. But the element of uncertainty in our knowledge of the external world make luck and risk intrinsic to all actions.

It is difficult to argue that the Enron case is one of bad moral luck. But other cases of corporate failure might be seen as unsuccessful gambles – the collapse of Barings Bank in the 1990s occurred when a trader built up huge positions on behalf of the company, and was brought down by external events over which he had no control. Not all unethical corporate actions have the intention of achieving an unethical end. Many result from poor risk analysis, lack of consideration of others, or an over-valuation of one's own situation. Even in the Enron case, one could imagine Lay saying 'I know it violates the rules, but I think that if the markets do not go badly against us everyone will win in the long run.' Of course such things are sometimes said as dishonest cover-ups of what someone knows to be wrong, but in this imaginary scenario, someone might argue that Lay acted as he did believing that he could eventually emerge without (any very great) ethically wrong outcomes. There is however another side to this, namely the poor judgement that results in a weak assessment of risks. The list of ethically wrong aspects of Lay's behaviour includes not only dishonesty and carelessness about the lives of others, but also that he took too great a risk – risk analysis and the judgement used in evaluating risks is thus subject to ethical evaluation. We learn from this, then, that all actions carry some level of moral luck, and that our estimation of risk may be a significant ethical element in itself.

Another aspect of Enron is that, although it is clear that Kenneth Lay and others were individually guilty of ethical wrongdoing, we do not refer to this as the Lay case, but as the Enron case. The company, as a collective, is seen as the actor.

We do find use for this idea of collective action – a strike by employees is an example of this. But not all collections of individual acts are a collective act – if everybody in an office happens, without reference to anyone else, to delete an email from the CEO, this is simply a lot of individual actions. Equally, a collective act does not mean that every member of that collective participated in the act. Some employees of Enron actively tried to avert the unethical choices, but although we might say that they were not blameworthy as individuals, the entity of which they were a member carried out the actions. Often membership of a firm is enough to say that someone has some responsibility for what happens, irrespective of their personal intentions. Someone who worked in an oil company and knew nothing of what was going on in another department is not as guilty as those whose actions led to a major oil spill, but they are not as blameless as someone who had never had any involvement with that company at all.

What underpins guilt by association? One aspect is psychological identification with the mission and activities of a company. If someone wholeheartedly supports their company's vision and operations, then implicitly they are approving of what is done in the name of the firm – almost 'my company right or wrong', even if they do not know exactly everything that has taken place; just as a member of a family is often held to be slightly 'tainted' if one of the family commits a serious crime. Another aspect is the suspicion of some kind of hidden instrumentality. If I work for a firm that acts unethically, even though I might not have directly worked towards the unethical act I might *indirectly* have contributed to it – I might have trained the guilty party, or approved the resourcing of the project in the course of which the unethical act happened. In this case I was unknowingly part of the cause of what has happened – one kind of bad moral luck. Further, I might not even have been part of *that particular* chain of causes, but the work I was doing might have contributed to what the offending team did, so it was 'only' good moral luck that on this specific occasion I did not directly cause what happened. A collective action is therefore not defined solely in terms of the intentions of the members of that community. And neither need all the members of the community be aware of the causality involved.

But nor is it also always a matter of the intentions of the members of the organisation. In UK law, and elsewhere, there is a phenomenon known as 'institutional' racism – meaning that an organisation *as a whole* discriminates against minority ethnic groups. But this does not imply that any *individual* does so. Possibly *no one at all* in the organisation is personally racist, but the configuration of policies and practices means that members of minority ethnic groups are disadvantaged in their dealings with the company. And though no individual is personally culpable for what happens, each member still shares the responsibility for what goes on.

One test of whether something is a collective act is whether either the staff or those affected by the action regard it as collective. However, they might be mistaken in this. Suppose an organisation's activities cause the destruction of part of the Brazilian rainforest, do we say that it is not a collective act if no one in the company thought it was so, claiming it was just a few 'bad apples'? Probably we would dismiss their views. Equally, if the local inhabitants also felt that this was not destruction by a company but just by a few of its employees we would still regard this as a collective action by the company.

Another possible test might be the source of the causality – if senior executives had promulgated the policy, and then middle level managers implemented it, and local supervisors put it into practice piecemeal, ending with the destruction of the rainforest – would this be a collective act, even when none of them connected up in their minds the destruction with the policy? This seems more plausible, but here too there are difficulties. Consider a company policy that usually brings great benefits to the local inhabitants of the rainforest – say planting a new species of a fast growing, healthy crop. But the very same week that the crop is planted, by a freak accident a volcanic eruption a hundred miles away deposits acidic dust on the crop, and this combines with natural chemical outputs of that crop (in themselves harmless) to poison the soil, killing off the surrounding woodlands. In this case we would still say that the company did, collectively, do something that destroyed that local environment, even if they had not meant to.

However, let's change this example – the eruption is not the week that the crops are planted, but twenty years later, and the same result occurs. In such a case the causality is the same, the moral luck is the same, and the policies are the same. But it seems less plausible to say that this is the action of the company. The only differences here are that the local inhabitants have enjoyed the benefit of the fast growing crops for some time, and quite likely many of the executives and managers in the company have retired, moved on to other jobs etc.

It is not simply that there has been a long time between what was done and its outcome. A company that buries a flask containing nuclear waste is responsible for estimating the likely consequences not just in five but also in five hundred years' time. And a fraud that is concealed for many years remains a fraud, even if legally some statute of limitations renders it no longer open to prosecution. And this is still a question of determining whether something is a corporate act – not (yet) a matter of who is to blame. But it does suggest that the definition of an action is bound up with whom it is deemed appropriate to consider blameworthy – not, note, who actually *is* to be blamed, but who is, as it were, in the ring for blame.

FREE ACTION

7.2 In the previous section we did not arrive at a complete definition of the idea of a collective action. There are, however, some further considerations that undermine the parallelism between a collective action and an individual one. We will look in this section at the idea of a free individual action.

Before doing this, note that specifying exactly what a particular action is can be ambiguous. Consider the following, which all might be legitimate reports of the same phenomenon:

- The manager uttered the word 'Yes'
- The manager agreed with the Chair of the Board
- The manager delivered a put-down to his rival
- The manager decided to dismiss two members of staff
- The manager sent a warning shot to the workforce about internal discipline.

It is easy to imagine a scenario where each of these is true of the same particular action. Yet they each have different content, defined in part by how much of the total outcome is taken as part of the action, and how much as external effect. It is implausible to say that the total set of effects of an act are what someone did. And equally it seems to misrepresent the situation to suggest that only someone's most basic bodily movements count as their action – in this scenario that probably would not even be the first statement, but one that described specifically the motions of someone's mouth and lips, and the amount of air that passed through. So how we identify someone's action is not always clear. Nor can we say that the action is what we intended – sometimes we are only dimly aware of the effects that we might bring about, and only dimly aware of what our 'true' intentions are. Be that as it may, in general people are held responsible for what they do and for its foreseeable results.

When an individual does something, in deciding whether they are responsible for it, we judge whether or not the event was something they chose freely. There may be several reasons why we excuse someone from responsibility. One might be physical compulsion – if I jostle someone because I accidentally slipped on the pavement, then although the event is annoying to others it is not my fault. Another issue might be coercion. If someone tells me that I have to lie to a client or else I and others will lose our jobs if that client cancels a contract, it might be alleged that I was forced into this. And finally if I have lost my rational faculty, my action is not deemed under my control. The most extreme version of this is when someone is suffering from a mental disorder. But in organisational life it is also common to excuse people's behaviour on account of their emotional state. Someone loses their temper and says things they should not have done, and then later excuses themselves on the ground of being stressed – and we accept this excuse.[1]

Now, although this is not a complete basis for all excuses, it does provide the foundation for much giving or withholding of blame. But more is involved than simply causality. Granted, the person who slips is not responsible for bumping into others, unless they were careless. Also we do not expect that someone suffering from a major mental disorder can do much about it. However, if someone is coerced, there appears to be a balance between the threat of harm that makes up the coercion, and the scale of the action that they are forced to do. Consider a person who is told to lie about the safety of an oil rig to a client who is thinking of leasing it, or else they and many others will lose their jobs. The lie might lead to people being seriously harmed and dying. In this case we might say that the loss of jobs, even many of them, is not sufficient to justify the lie. If on the other hand the lie refers to the capacity a firm has to deliver stationery by a certain date, then we might feel less strongly – the threat might be accepted as excusing the lie.

---

[1] Whilst it is the case that sometimes such an apology is offered just to keep the peace, in principle at least it is accepted that a mood or temper can disarm someone's normal rational faculties.

Similarly, when someone 'loses' their temper, we assume that a certain level of control is still there – if they have been told they have been sacked, then it might be acceptable for them to shout or cry, but it would not be acceptable to throw a table through a window: there remain presumed boundaries over which the person has some control, even if within those boundaries it might be accepted that they relinquish some of their self-restraint.

The point about these examples is not which issues may be accepted as mitigation of an individual's action, but that *mitigation takes place at all*. We accept some factors as mitigating to some extent – the bigger the factor the greater the mitigation. In such cases an individual, then, can be taken as sometimes not being responsible for their actions, but otherwise they are deemed to have *freely chosen* to do what they did.

There is a long running issue about what 'free action' means. Assuming that in principle we can have a complete scientific explanation of the observable world – including human behaviour – then for any action that takes place there would be an explanation that shows how that was caused. But how can I be said to have 'freely' chosen, if it can be proved that my choice was the outcome of a chain of causes? Would I then be as determined by natural laws as the rocks and waves? There are several options here – one is to accept that freedom is a complete illusion, another to deny that science can form a complete picture of human decisions. An alternative is that science and agency are two different kinds of conceptualisation and do not conflict with each other – for example, so-called 'soft' determinism claims that a scientific explanation may be complete but this is compatible with our experience of weighing up decisions and making choices. Another related view is that a scientific explanation codifies the factors that we use when we make choices, but does not imply that there is anything outside those factors compelling us to act in certain ways. Especially interesting is Kant's view that scientific explanation only works on material that we access through experience, whereas the sense of freedom we have to weigh up reasons and make choices operates at a *super-sensible* level; in other words that our experience of ourselves as actors is not through the senses, but is access to something as it is in itself.

Whatever the precise resolution of this dilemma, it seems clear that notwithstanding the assumption of the completeness of scientific explanation, we still feel that we can attribute freedom to people's choices – or that they were *not* free, for one of the mitigating reasons given earlier.

COLLECTIVE ACTIONS

7.3 Do we have the same kind of distinction when it comes to a collective, organisational action?

Consider where a financial company sells products from other firms – such as an insurance broker selling investment schemes from a major bank.

Suppose that the bank's schemes were in fact corrupt – known by bank officials to be faulty and likely to lose investors money but still garner good profits for the bank. Suppose also that the insurance broker does not know this. Then even in such a case, although the broker firm is not fully responsible for what happened, and it did not carry out the fraud, nevertheless the firm was not completely devoid of all responsibility, since we would have expected it to have exercised some diligence in checking that the schemes were sound. The sheer presence in the chain of causes implies some involvement, and a lack of direct knowledge does not mitigate all responsibility.

This suggests that even where a company does not fulfil one of the key necessary conditions for an action to be deemed entirely free (that they know what the effects of their actions will be) nevertheless it is not completely excused responsibility for what happens. This seems to indicate a higher standard of responsibility for corporations than for individuals. With individual action, if someone is deprived of knowledge about a situation then their responsibility for what happens is diminished if not entirely removed. But with a corporation the assumption is that they are responsible not only for what happens but also *for how much knowledge they have*.

There is a further issue with the idea of a collective action. With human beings, it is accepted that sometimes they know what is the thing to do but the act itself is difficult to carry through – perhaps because it involves some real or imagined unpleasantness. And if it is too unpleasant our resolve might fail us. *We sometimes have weak wills.* Can we say the same thing about a corporate action? The closest analogy might be that an organisation has a stated policy to do x, but for various reasons does not manage to implement this. Mintzberg talks of 'emergent'[2] strategy – that explicit strategic choices are not always the sole determinant of what a corporation actually ends up doing. Is this weakness one of corporate will?

Consider a government health service that at the highest level decides that all people within a certain age-range should be screened for a certain disease. Such a strategic choice is then rolled out to local offices to be implemented. Now suppose we come back a year later and find that hardly anyone in that age group has been screened, despite the overall strategic decision. Do we say that the organisation tried but did not have the will to do this? It does not sound plausible. More plausible is to say that the organisation as a whole was not committed to the strategic decision. In other words this was less a failure of will than a case where the decision had not been consolidated.

The idea of the corporate agent, then, does not seem to parallel the human person exactly – for we accept a level of fallibility with people that we do not with corporations. So whilst it is a convenient simplification, such an idea is useful but not able to cover all cases adequately.

---

[2]Mintzberg, H. *The Rise and Fall of Strategic Planning: Reconceiving Roles for Planning, Plans, Planners* (The Free Press, 1994).

THE DESIRE–BELIEF MODEL OF ACTION

7.4 The issue of weakness of will just considered raises another interesting aspect of human action. A common view of action is that it results from the combination of desires and beliefs. We want outcome x, and we believe that action a is an effective route to achieve x, so we do a. In management theory this is the root of the theory of motivation known as *expectancy theory,* or sometimes *valency theory,* propounded originally by Victor Vroom. In philosophy it is sometimes referred to as the desire–belief model or even the instrumental model of action, and goes back at least to the time of David Hume.

This model might be thought to predict which kinds of actions are most likely to be adopted by individuals. I am much more attracted to the idea of becoming the prime minister of my country, than to getting promoted to becoming departmental head of my company. But given the extremely low probability of the former in comparison with the latter, I am more likely to make moves to getting the promotion than going for the political career.

The idea that motive is constructed of the interplay between desires and beliefs depicts an action as the natural outcome of such a combination. There are however difficulties with this view. Often we *cannot* predict what someone will do on the basis of their desires and beliefs, because it is their *behaviour* that provides us with the evidence of these. If I suddenly resign from my job and join a political party, then it would be *on that basis* that people inferred that I had a strong desire to have a political career. If I stayed in my job, no matter how strongly I expressed this desire to go into politics, it would be inferred that I did not *really* desire it very strongly after all. The same point can be made about what I believe. Someone who says that the ice is safe to walk on, but does not walk on it themselves, does not really believe this. In other words, often we infer from behaviour to beliefs and desires, not from beliefs and desires to behaviour. A further complication here is with the idea of a 'desire' or want. There is a sense in which, if I did something at all, I must have wanted it in some way. But this is not the same as suggesting that any *particular* kind of inner motivating state, such as a drive, was present. This does not refute the desire–belief model, it only renders it not very useful for predicting behaviour.

In practice, many actions that individuals take are a *compromise* between different wants, and different estimations of the likelihood of certain outcomes. Consider two senior managers having a heated dispute in a management meeting. In each case there is a cluster of different desires, and of different beliefs about what might happen. There is not only the desire to win the argument, the wish to seem decisive in front of the Chief Executive, the wish to look forceful in front of subordinates, but also the desire not to look foolish, or overly bullying, and so on. And similarly there is a cluster of uncertainties about what might actually result from the exchange, and what that result could lead to. In many situations there is a weighing up of these different wishes and uncertainties, often with little time or space for deliberation. Many courses of action are also taken specifically because they keep future options open, as well as steering the progress of events through several different possible sets of outcomes that are more or less desirable.

So whilst it might not be false to say that eventually, when someone does decide what to do, that might be analysed as:

desire + belief –> action

The reality that leads to this is more complex, and looks more like:

[cluster of desires] –> most dominant configuration of these
+
[cluster of beliefs] –> most likely of these
=> action

We have seen also that will is sometimes weak, and whilst that is probably down to the strength of one set of desires over another, the fact that sometimes people can make an effort and overcome their fears, suggests that the complex of wishes and desires that leads to this is not the stable state of a person, but a fluctuating cluster which may change depending on which possible outcomes are considered.

The desire–belief model creates an impression of being an instrument of action, as if action is a mechanistic result of the desire–belief complex in question. We have seen some shortcomings with this – the episodic or even ephemeral nature of some of these desires and beliefs, as well as the fact that some acts are not simple moves towards a particular end but navigating through a trail of potential outcomes. Even in a brief encounter such as a corridor exchange between managers, the actions that the protagonists take may be better considered as more like journeys towards a desired end than a completed event.

PRACTICAL REASON

7.5 The term 'practical reason' originated as a translation of what Aristotle called *phronesis* (which he distinguished from theoretical reason, the search for truth). In Aristotle's sense, practical reason was the progress of deliberation to action – he was specific that it is an *action* not an intention that is the conclusion of practical reasoning. Aristotle was also explicit that practical reason applies to the means to achieve ends, and that ends themselves are not subjects for this kind of consideration. This would seem to place him in with the desire–belief category, but it is worth noting that the examples he gives (the end, for a doctor of healing people, or for a statesman of producing law and order) seem less to be objects of wants and more like *policies*, long-term ends.

Hume, though he did not use the phrase 'practical reason', had a similar view of the relationship between our cognitive faculties and our motives – famously arguing that 'reason is, and only ever can be, the slave of the passions'. In asserting this, he countered those who argued that reason can determine the ends of action. Hume argued that reasoning only ever deals with 'relations of ideas' or 'matters of fact' and therefore no action can come about simply because of our reasoning. There had to be some other factor involved, the motivating force – the passions, as he called them.

Kant discussed practical reason extensively, and in the case of morality explicitly rejected Hume's instrumental view. He, like Aristotle, argued that there is a direct linkage between practical reason and *action,* but he drew quite different conclusions from this. His conception of practical reason is more subtle, but it is based on the idea that reason, in his sense, is the search for fundamental elements, and hence practical reason is the search for what is a fundamental, unconditioned, basis for action. In Kant's case there were two different manifestations of practical reason. *Empirical* practical reason was the instrumental link between ends and the means to achieve these. *Pure* practical reason determines an imperative for action that applies to rational beings irrespective of what they happen to desire. [3]

What is important in this idea of practical reason, in either a Kantian or Aristotelian sense, is that it goes beyond just the calculation of what means will achieve what ends. Practical reason is the *harnessing* of reasoning to intent or desire. Whereas for Hume 'practical reason' means something like 'reason that deals with ideas for which we have some passion', for both Kant and Aristotle practical reason means the movement of reason towards action: for Kant it led to an imperative (*not* a statement of what means will lead to what end, but a statement expressing motive force) whilst for Aristotle this led to the action itself. This does not on its own directly contradict Hume. But it has a different nuance. Practical reason, in this sense, terminates in *action*, not in a statement. Hence it places the agent as directly engaged with the reality in which the action takes place, rather than with the representation of that reality in a stated conclusion.

What relevance does this have to action in organisations? Deliberation, in an organisation, takes many forms – in the case of long-term or wide ranging choices it might involve consultancy reports, analysis of performance data etc. However, not all of these count as genuine processes of practical reason. Consider a government department with a politically embarrassing problem – say the immigration department has failed to prevent some tourists

---

[3]And, as we shall see in the next chapter, what Kant identified as the supreme principle of morality.

from overstaying their visas, and so they have become illegal migrants. The government minister might order a report into the matter, specifying that recommendations need to be formulated to prevent this recurring and insisting that 'lessons will be learnt'. If the inquiry is instituted simply to reassure the public that 'something is being done', and the minister will only act on the report if it agrees with her/his own views, then this is not deliberation at all. If, however, the minister intends to implement the recommendations of the report, if they are reasonably acceptable, then it could well be an example of practical reason proper. The difference is that if the inquiry is not intended to change policy then it is not a piece of practical reason whereas if it is set up in the belief that it *might* change policy then it is genuinely practical reasoning – even if eventually the decision is taken not to act on the recommendations. A great deal of apparent investigation in management is what might be called pseudo-practical reason – consultancy exercises and reports that are not intended to lead to action but are done to go through the motions of investigation, or even simply lend credibility to management prejudices.

On this view, admittedly some way beyond what Kant and Aristotle argued, being practical is not a definitive property of a sequence of reasoning, but represents a scale – from reason that is definitely going to result in action at the end (e.g. a panel deliberating as to whom of a set of external applicants to appoint to a brand new position in the firm) through to reasoning that is hardly practical at all, even though it might be dressed up to look more practical than it really is (such as a consultancy report to justify a decision that has already been taken by a senior manager to close down a certain department).

A more important issue is that when we say that an individual did something, we can indicate directly the locus of the act, a point which acts as the destination of any praise or blame that might attach to the action in question. An organisation is not, however, a point – there are departments, individuals, potentially conflicting actors within the firm, so that it is only a fiction devised by legal authorities and others to treat the action of a collective in the same manner as one might the action of an individual.

SPACE AND ACTION

7.6 In an interview with Paul Rabinow,[4] the French philosopher Michel Foucault emphasises the role that space plays in our thinking and action. The organisation of space in the city, for example, reflects assumptions about human activity, and channels that activity in certain ways – town planning is in effect also political and social planning. Furthermore, how

---

[4]"Space Knowledge and Power' reprinted in *The Foucault Reader*, ed. P. Rabinow (Penguin, 1991) pp. 239–56.

space is used in our processes of representation of situations reflects assumptions about what is represented: Foucault uses the example in biology of how spatial representations of plants in the seventeenth century, via drawings and diagrams, reflected and encouraged a certain visually based approach to the plant, and correspondingly discouraged other approaches.

Such a perspective also tells us a lot about the structure of action in an organisation. The division of large office spaces into half-closed cubicles, for example, depicts the worker and their acts as public but individual. The enclosure of the manager – often in a corner office but with large windows out on to the 'open plan' space of the team – denotes separation from and ascendancy over the rest of the team. Paradoxically, the lack of enclosure facilitates overseeing, but there is no real space for collective collaborative discussion and decision making.

The classical diagrammatic representation of an organisation is a tree, with the most senior members of staff at the very top, at the apex of a pyramid, going down to a wide base, of front line staff. This plays a significant part in decision making: the pyramid is seen as a metaphor for many things – authority, (often) pay levels, and career tracks, as well as communications. In deliberating about what to do, the typical staff member thinks in the first instance of going 'upward' to seek authorisation, and only latterly, if at all, in going 'sideways' to seek the potential collaborative opportunities from colleagues. 'Downward' communication is usually imagined as a form of gravitational pull on decisions that have already been made higher up, and need to be 'cascaded' (a favoured managerial term) through the structure.

The organisational tree embodies power relationships, but also this *spatialisation* (to use Foucault's term) of organisations plays an important role in how practical reason can operate. The channelling process at work in the tree image, whilst not *determining* what is thought or done, plays a significant role. One interesting aspect of the organisational tree is that in larger and more complex corporations the key individuals who provide the basic rationale for the organisation existing at all – its clients or customers – are completely missing. This reflects that organisations rarely have systematic processes of decision making that include their clientele. So much so that additional artificial processes such as focus groups, or consultative panels, are set up to feed in to senior management decision making.

ACTIONS, OUTCOMES AND EXPRESSIONS

7.7 One final point to note about action is to return to the model of intention–action–outcome. We have seen earlier that intentions do relate to expected outcomes, but not in a clear one-to-one correspondence. Some outcomes cannot be foreseen clearly; with others no reasonable estimate can be made; sometimes the possible outcomes are too complex to understand, and sometimes we do not even fully understand our own motives. So whilst intentions are linked to what we expect will result from our acts they cannot be identified with these. Blame, therefore, which generally is linked to the results of what we do, carries this element which earlier we called moral luck.

What is rarely considered in discussions of managerial decision making is the fact that not all action is undertaken because it will achieve a *result*. Sometimes people act in a certain way because they want to *express* something. This is not to say that there is no anticipated outcome – someone may hope, say, that they will achieve satisfaction from having 'expressed' something by acting in a certain way, or that they demonstrate to others a certain attitude. But the primary intent of such an act is not the succeeding chain of causes and effects, but the fact that the action represents a certain kind of event.

A different kind of 'expressiveness' may be seen in the case of mergers and acquisitions. It is acknowledged academically that mergers and acquisitions frequently fail to achieve their stated strategic intentions – merger costs are often higher than anticipated, the acquired firm is not as profitable as due diligence seemed to indicate, or the process of merging different workforces and resources is more difficult than was originally supposed, and so on. Yet despite this knowledge being widespread, business school educated managers still continue with buying and disposing of companies at sometimes alarming rates. It could in some cases be attributed to a simple need for power or prestige, in which case this is a clear intention to achieve that specific outcome. But additionally, growing to dominate an industry sector can be seen – admittedly rather speculatively – as a means of expression of the vitality and muscle of an organisation.

BOX 7.1

AN EXPRESSIVE MANAGEMENT ACTION

Consider again the so-called open-plan office, which is really a series of small individualised spaces that inhibit free and open discussion on business issues. Whilst this may have been evaluated in terms of worker efficiency, such arrangements 'speak volumes' about the attitudes of senior management to their staff. Whilst we cannot directly infer anything about the conscious intention of the manager who decided on the plan, the outcome plays a role in everyone's conception of the way that office works.

Similarly, in an industry niche dominated by a small number of players (retail petrol companies in a specific country for example) the periodic price wars that regularly ensue have little positive impact on long-term profitability. In the short term one or other player gains an improvement in market share, but the cut in prices means that profits do not rise in parallel with this, and in any case the other players usually catch up relatively soon, and gradually these key players let the prices float upwards to their previous point. What has happened? One interpretation of this is that the price war is a reminder that the players are in competition – a price war is less of a rational market-capturing strategy and more of a psychological move 'against' one's fellow traders. Doubtless this analogy cannot be taken too far, but it underlines that some business strategies are not adopted for their results.

In this chapter we have looked at several aspects of action. In particular, we have found that:

- In all acts there is some element of risk – or even of *moral luck.*
- Guilt, and hence blame, is sometimes attributed to us, not by our role in a sequence of events, but by association.
- Whilst it can be convenient to talk of collective actions, some aspects of individual human agency, such as freedom of choice, or weakness of will, do not apply.
- Some actions may be less to do with rational calculation and more to do with expression.

In the following chapter we will look more specifically at the idea of *right* – ethically right – actions, and the various theories relating to this concept.

QUESTIONS FOR CONSOLIDATION

1   What ways are there for depicting diagrammatically an organisation, alternative to the 'tree' hierarchy? What do these say about the power relationships in the firm?

2   Consider a major disaster, such as a tsunami or earthquake. How far would this exonerate a company from the consequences of, say, the emission of poisonous gas as a result of the turmoil involved?

FURTHER READING

Aristotle, *Nichomachean Ethics* (Penguin Classics, 2004) Jonathan Barnes (Introduction), J. A. K. Thomson (Translator).

Hume, D. (1740) *Treatise of Human Nature* (Oxford University Press, 2011), edited D. F. Norton and M. J. Norton.

Kant, I. (1788) *Critique of Practical Reason* (Cambridge University Press, 1997), edited M. J. Gregor, introduction by A. Reath.

THEORIES OF BUSINESS ETHICS

In the previous chapter we looked at action in general – the ideas of collective action, human freedom and the mitigation of personal responsibility, and the boundaries between acts and their consequences.

This chapter does not aim to replicate the content of the many texts on business ethics. Rather the intention is to focus on the fundamental philosophical theories of goodness that underpin ethical debates.

When you have finished this chapter, you should be able to:

- identify a model of action that highlights the main emphases of the key ethical theories
- critically evaluate the strengths and weaknesses of three key theories of ethics
- apply theories effectively to typical business dilemmas.

BOX 8.1

THREE BUSINESS ETHICS DILEMMAS

1. Alan, a university lecturer, is offered a present of an expensive watch by a grateful student. College rules prohibit accepting expensive gifts, but Alan does not want to upset the feelings of the student.
2. Lief is a purchasing manager who discovers that a major supplier in a developing country is exploiting young children. He investigates but although he feels sure that there is something wrong none of the children will complain, and many of the parents approve of their children working.
3. Lee is a popular supervisor. One of his team, Tina, reveals that she witnessed Sam, a colleague, taking tools out of the factory, but he then forced her to look after them overnight. Lee should report this, but if he does so Tina may be implicated.

SOME KEY DILEMMAS IN BUSINESS

8.1 Consider the examples in Box 8.1.

In Dilemma 1 both parties are motivated by the value of respect in professional life. However, for one respect is a personal matter, whilst for the other it requires some symbolic material manifestation to be regarded as genuine. This is not a problematic dilemma to resolve – Alan has several options which should help him out of his difficulty, such as accepting the gift but straightaway donating it to the college hardship fund, or disclosing it to his manager, who can then decide how to dispose of it.

With Dilemma 2 there may be a difference in the interpretation of 'exploitation'. But there are also factual issues. Have the children been primed to say that they are happy? Do the parents fear that things might get worse if they tell the truth? In evaluating these, Lief is not just making a cognitive judgement, he is also making a moral commitment. If he decides to accept the children's views at face value, he then takes a risk that, if wrong, he may have assisted in the exploitation. Similarly if he rejects their view, he may undermine their job security. In ethical contexts, cognitive positions are not just a mechanical outcome of evidence and reasoning. Because there are generally so many uncertainties in real life, they also represent ethical positions.

With Dilemma 3, the interpretation of the key values of honesty and trust is not in question. And despite uncertainty about the actual outcomes, there is a reasonable probability (a) that the tools were stolen and (b) that Sam might victimise Tina in some way. Less clear, though potentially significant, is whether company disciplinary proceedings might also implicate Tina, even though Lee believes that she intended no dishonesty.

The resolution of this dilemma is more difficult. Lee is unlikely to find a solution that respects the integrity of the firm without implicating Tina. One route out of this might be to persuade Tina to go to senior management and report what she knows, though this may expose herself to retaliation by Sam as well as being accused of complicity. Another might be to insist that Sam return the tools, promising that if he leaves immediately and does not retaliate against Tina then he will not be reported to the police. The risks for Lee with this option are significant, but the final outcome may be easier for all parties.

What do these cases tell us about ethical dilemmas in business? Firstly, options for action may violate one value in order to satisfy another. Secondly, a value may be shared by different parties, but their *interpretations* of it may differ. Thirdly, the resolution of factual uncertainties in business ethics dilemmas can often be an ethical action, not just a cognitive judgement. And finally, some creativity is often needed to resolve a dilemma.

A further point concerns people's fundamental orientation to ethics. Even in straightforward cases, people will rarely aim to do wrong deliberately. Socrates may have gone too far when he claimed (according to Plato) that 'no one ever knowingly does evil', but often wrong is done in the belief that it is right. We might judge some event on the basis of its outcomes without knowing salient details of the agent's situation, or of the impact of a certain event on its stakeholders, perhaps assuming incorrectly that their reaction would be the same as our own. And even in cases where there is no dispute over either facts or values, it can be unclear whether someone has done right or wrong at all – for example when someone is 'cruel to be kind'.

ETHICAL ISSUES IN BUSINESS

8.2 Fundamental to ethics in business is the clash between two sets of values. For organisations to succeed, they need to fulfil their mission and satisfy those who direct and govern them. On the other hand, the individuals and groups who are involved in or affected by the organisation's operations have a right to be treated in an acceptable manner. Many key ethical issues arise out of this potential conflict between organisational performance, and treating people decently.

There is an argument that 'good ethics is good business' but this is often misunderstood. At best good ethics can only be a *necessary* condition of good business – some ethical moves do not work commercially, so it is not sufficient simply to act ethically, to ensure good business outcomes. But even so, this assumes that in the long term ethical features of people's behaviour in corporations will be identified and rewarded (or punished) as appropriate. And this in turn assumes (a) that in the long term the relevant evidence about people's behaviour will be discovered and (b) that when this happens people will still care enough about the issues to deal with them. In practice neither of these two assumptions is always borne out. Regrettably, we cannot appeal to business effectiveness to define what would count as ethically acceptable action.

This does not mean that there is nothing at all in the 'good ethics – good business' slogan. When ethically unacceptable actions *are* discovered then this can lead to a loss of trust or worse amongst key stakeholders. For example, in Britain during the 2000s, it was widely suspected that newspapers, especially the *News of the World*, were illegally hacking into the private phone and email accounts of individuals to get stories. But generally the political establishment and the public were not especially concerned, until it was revealed that the paper might have hacked into the phone of a young girl after she had been kidnapped and murdered. The ethical outrage concerning this led to great attention being given to phone hacking by journalists, the paper itself was shut down, and the editor and proprietor were taken to task in public enquiries. The discovery of one unethical act thus led to greater public concern about other acts of the paper, and breaches of privacy that hitherto had been dismissed were taken more seriously. The point is that a series of acts that if true were clearly illegal were not seen as particularly worrisome, until an action that was more seriously wrong became known, and then this led to a change in the attitude taken to the company. Perhaps the slogan really should be 'do wrong and it might damage your business', which is weaker, but still a useful cautionary note for executives.

The argument above implies that some issues that are treated as part of business ethics are properly speaking not *business* ethical issues at all, but *just ethical ones*. Whilst the Enron case is one both of bad business and bad ethics, if the intention of Lay and his associates was pure personal gain, then it is not a case of *business* ethics at all, but just of ethics plain and simple. If someone steals from a company, then it is just wrong. It does not need to be considered in the light of occurring in a business. If, on the other hand, this happens because the individual has witnessed more senior staff suggesting that this is acceptable, it is no less immoral, but this places it more into a business ethical context.

So we can divide ethical issues as they appear in business into two camps:

- ethical issues *in* business: such as bullying, racial or sexual abuse of staff, theft, accepting bribes, nepotism
- ethical issues *about* business: such as paying low wages to staff, governing an organisation improperly, offering bribes, charging unfair prices, misleading investors.

Some cases might fall into either category: with bribery it may be offered to benefit a business, or accepted for personal benefit. Similarly, someone might bully staff out of sheer inhumanity, or because they genuinely think this will lead to higher performance, in which case it could arguably be in the 'about' category.

The point is that some ethically blameworthy things happen in organisations just because people are there and, unfortunately, sometimes people act unethically. Some other things that are unethical, though, happen *because of* the context being business – business creates ethical challenges that go beyond the 'normal' issues we face in all aspects of our life. A male manager who expects his younger female subordinates to dress attractively for his pleasure is simply acting unethically. A manager who expects his younger female subordinates to dress attractively because he thinks this will be good for cementing good relationships with the firm's clients is violating *business* ethics.

For cases that raise solely ethical issues *in* business, there is nothing especially business-focused about them. They are ethical issues plain and simple. Someone who takes money from their employer is stealing. The response to such acts is clear – it is an offence and merits blame and, where appropriate, punishment.

Ethical issues *about* business are harder to deal with. Paying a senior executive a huge salary, when they put in no more time and/or effort working than a cleaner on the minimum wage, is indeed ethically questionable. It seems to militate against ideals of fairness. But arguably it might be central to the needs of a business. Such an issue is thus distinguished from theft or bullying, which generally are not necessary for a business to thrive. Not that all such ethical infringements are genuinely requirements of the business. Indeed, probably often they are not. What matters is that sometimes they could be.

These two categories require different responses. An individual who steals from their employer may be dealt with by, for example, punishment or restorative justice. To deal with an individual who lies to investors to improve company profits involves *rebalancing* the way they think of moral and business imperatives. The offence *about* business arises because the offender thinks that they are doing what the business requires. This does not apply to the individual who just steals or bullies. But believing in such a linkage is not a justification – indeed what it amounts to is the moral offence of taking something other than the good as of fundamental value. If anything it compounds the offence, for there are two blameworthy things involved – the lie to investors, as well as the judgement that business is more important than morals.

WHAT DOES 'ETHICALLY GOOD' MEAN IN AN ORGANISATIONAL CONTEXT?

8.3 There has been a long philosophical debate about what 'good' means, and how we can determine ethical issues. Some have argued that ethical arguments cannot be reduced to discussions about the facts. Hume famously claimed that you cannot derive an 'ought' from an 'is' – there is always a value statement involved as well. On the other hand, some have argued that stealing *just is* the act of taking property from others without permission and with the intention of keeping it: in other words that it is a factual matter after all. This has led to contrasting 'naturalistic' and 'non-naturalistic' explanations of moral language.

There are practical implications of these theoretical differences that affect the ways that firms manage ethics. For example, if moral values are 'natural' in character, then ethical development in an organisation involves making people more aware of consequences, and developing their ability to reason. In contrast, if someone held morality to be, say, an emotion, then the emphasis would be on how they feel about certain situations.

In practice many organisations adopt a hybrid strategy that appeals to sympathy and 'what if it were me?' scenarios, but also addresses people's reasoning about action. There is nothing intellectually or practically wrong with such approaches. But it is worth noting that implicitly they assume a mixed view of morality – that somehow it is *both* a factual/cognitive matter *and* an expressive or emotive one.

Is there something specific, theoretically, about what we are more narrowly calling ethics about business? One feature that is specific to business ethics is this link between what is morally right and what is good for the firm. It is misleading to see business interests or moral interests as *alternatives*. Moral values have an absolute authority. Whilst an individual may give priority to the needs of a business rather than to what is morally right, that does not mean that we cannot judge what is done on moral grounds. It was not open to Nike, for example, to say about their use of child labour in Pakistan in the 1990s 'Well, this is commercially very profitable for us, so we decided that ethics didn't apply here.' Such a claim would not, logically, counter an evaluation of their acts as ethically wrong. Ethics cannot be trumped by other factors, even though people may give it a lower priority. So it is not really a question of *balancing* ethics and other considerations. The issue is rather more how ethical considerations arise within the context of business interests.

'Ethical' therefore, in a business context, refers to the moral issues that are integral to the strategy and operations of the organisation, the manner in which business aims and operations are subject to moral evaluation. A business may have praiseworthy aims, and an ethically sound approach to key processes such as sourcing materials or managing workers, and yet still have many cases of individual ethically wrong acts such as bribery, or individual discrimination. This, in itself, does not make the business an unethical one – though it would cast doubt on the firm's approach to ethics if nothing were ever done about such infringements of moral values.

THE MODEL OF ACTION REVISITED

8.4 In Chapter 7 we discussed a model of action that focused on intentions, acts and outcomes. We saw, however, that this has grey areas – acts and intentions are sometimes defined in terms of their consequences. For the purposes of categorising ethical theories we will modify this model, to include a reference to what is prior to the formation of an intention, as diagrammatically represented below.

We shall look at three different areas of focus on what is the foundation of ethically right action – a focus on the consequences of the action, a focus

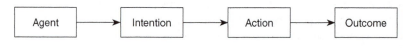

FIGURE 8.1

on the actions themselves, and finally a focus on the nature of an agent and the moral elements in the character traits they possess.

A cautionary note needs to be sounded about these focuses. As theories of what is right or wrong, they are *analyses* of the concept. It is tempting to regard them as *alternative ways to justify an action*. However, if one is searching for ways to justify one's act, one cannot use one theory, and if that does not supply the desired justification, then try some other way. This makes each of the theories we examine below look like tools to be adopted as required. This is misleading, and we will return to this at the end of the chapter.

THE FOCUS ON OUTCOMES

8.5 The focus on the outcomes of an action as determining whether it is ethically right is known as *consequentialism*. On this view, an action is justified if it produces on balance good outcomes. Given that actions, especially in a corporate environment, produce many different results, it becomes necessary to (a) identify these, (b) evaluate each against some fundamental standard as being morally good or bad, and (c) combine them to generate a summary of the rightness or wrongness of an act.

Although versions of consequentialism were developed in ancient China,[1] the best known version of this, *utilitarianism*, was developed in the nineteenth century by the English philosophers Jeremy Bentham and John Stuart Mill. Utilitarianism identifies the external standard of evaluation as pleasure, or happiness, and proposes that the combined outcomes of an action should be evaluated on the basis of 'the greatest happiness of the greatest number'.[2]

This principle works by evaluating different options – the right action is the one that produces the most happiness. In the case of Lee and Tina, for example, each option available to Lee is evaluated in terms of the total happiness produced by its outcomes, and a comparison of these summaries will indicate which is the right one to adopt.

There are some interesting applications of the consequentialist approach. A utilitarian approach to punishment, for example, emphasises the *outcome* of the practice – that it should deter people in general, not just the offending individual, from breaking the rules. In some cases this might be by setting very high sanctions for breaking the rules, so that people are deterred by fear. In others it might be by providing positive benefits as an incentive to comply with rules.

---

[1]The philosopher Mozi, writing in the 5th century BCE, advocated a form of consequentialism focused on what would protect and enhance the good of the state.

[2]Against the objection that this suggests that morality is no more than *hedonism*, Mill argued that the theory does not identify pleasures as being of equal value – there are 'higher' pleasures and 'lower' ones.

In practice, there are difficulties with consequentialism, as a methodology for deciding what to do:

- we often don't consider all the options
- we often cannot work out all the consequences of an action
- whether a particular action will lead to a particular consequence always carries a degree of uncertainty
- some consequences cannot be easily compared with each other.

Whilst these do not refute consequentialism, they make it less useful than it would appear at first sight. There are also other philosophical weaknesses with the approach. Imagine a company that has been publicly revealed as being involved in a major scandal. To admit the extent of the scandal might bring the whole firm down, with the loss of many jobs. But to make an example of one person, sack them publicly and blame all the problems on them, will save the company. From a consequentialist point of view, this option seems to provide the greatest happiness of the greatest number, but for many of us the unfairness of the treatment of whoever is scapegoated for the scandal would not be right. More is going on, therefore, in our ethical judgements than simply estimating outcomes. Some actions just seem more fair than others.

Another objection is that consequentialism seems to require us to take an objective view of all outcomes, whether they affect us directly or not. Anyone in possession of the same information about outcomes of an action would come to the same conclusion, on this view, because all actions are evaluated in terms of their contribution to the common good. This requires each agent to act as if they were an ideal actor, unswayed by their own affiliations. Hume pointed out, however, that we are affected by *moral distance*. We tend to value those closest to us physically, genetically, and personally, more than those with whom we have no connection. Hume exaggerated when he said that it would make no difference to me if someone far distant, unknown and unrelated to me were destroyed, but generally it will matter much less than if this happened to someone I know well. This echoes the notion of *guanxi* – the Chinese tradition of preferring to work with those with whom one has a personal association.

The assumption of altruism conflicts with modern economic theory, which is based on the idea that the pursuit of one's personal interest is the most effective way to increase the general wealth of a society. However, this conflict can arguably be countered by the version of consequentialism that applies, not to specific actions, but to *rules* for action. On this view, it is the rule that is justified by whether it increases human happiness, not every individual action. However, rule-consequentialism, it might be argued, can be seen as less of a focus on the results of actions, and more on the nature of actions themselves, given that the justification of such rules is often highly projective.

Overall, consequentialism, despite its appearance of practical application, does not always provide a clear guide as to what should be done.

THE FOCUS ON ACTIONS

8.6 Moving from a focus on the results, let us consider the focus on actions themselves. As we saw when discussing consequentialism, some actions are just unfair, even when the total balance of results is good for the majority. This implies that something other than outcomes is at least part of how we evaluate actions. Some actions in themselves are part of our moral duty. This category of a theory of ethics is often called *deontology*, from the Greek word 'deon' meaning a duty.

Some deontological theories focus on the agent, and their duties, while others focus on those affected by actions – victims, beneficiaries and their rights. But they share the claim that we ought to do some things simply because it is our duty to do so. Telling the truth, say, is always a good thing to do; murdering someone is always wrong. This view abstracts from consequences, and looks at the action itself. However, it would be misleading to suggest that, on a deontological theory, outcomes have nothing whatsoever to do with morality. As we saw in the previous chapter, it is not possible to draw a clear line between intentions, behaviour and outcomes. And it is impossible to even define murder without referring to the outcome that someone has been killed.

Examples of the kind of action that a deontologist might point to in business could include: telling customers the truth about a service even when that might lead them to shop elsewhere or allowing a member of the team time off from work due to personal distress, even when this creates problems for the other team members. Doubtless these *might* be done as a result of a calculation of results. But the deontological point is that such actions ought to be done irrespective of outcomes – on the grounds simply that they are the right things to do. As Kant put it, a moral action is one that is done for the sake of duty. And a duty is not negotiable – it may be over-ruled in fact, but it cannot be dismissed.

What though is the source of such duties? What justifies us saying that telling the truth is a duty (as opposed, say, from justifying it on a consequentialist basis that it brings about the best outcomes)? One such justification might be religious, though this can hardly account for the ethics of non-believers. Some twentieth-century philosophers talked of the goodness of an action being a 'non-natural' property. Arguably, however, this is simply an artificial abstraction, which makes debate problematic, for what counts as evidence of a 'non-natural' phenomenon? In a professional context such a position would have little appeal, though it is likely that this kind of view is not intended to make people more inclined to choose ethically right actions, but simply to explain what we mean when we say that something is right or wrong.

In this respect the rights-based version of deontology has a simpler case, in that it can refer to the fundamental features of humanity as the basis of duty. Though it is not usually presented as a theory of deontological ethics, the conception of justice developed by John Rawls is not dependent on out-comes. To over-simplify his views, he suggested that we judge whether a certain arrangement of wealth[3] is just or not, by assuming that we might occupy *any* position in that arrangement – from the best to the worst: if the worst is still tolerable, then implicitly we are accepting that arrangement as just, whereas if the worst position is intolerable, then we are judging it as unfair.

On this view many of us might view some companies and government bodies as unfair. Consider the lot of an individual who works at or below the legal minimum wage, whose working environment is not protected in line with health and safety legislation, and who has no effective say in the requirements of their job. For most of us this falls below what we would regard as minimally acceptable. And thus, on Rawls' view, it would count as unfair.

One very general issue with this approach is that it assumes that we *can* understand what it is like to be in the worst position in society. Even when someone is not self-deceived, there are limits to what we can imagine, and the lot of those much less fortunate than ourselves may be such an example. Further, across the globe people's senses of what is acceptable vary widely – as we saw in Chapter 6, the very fundamentals of how individuals think can diverge in very basic ways. At best then, 'what we find acceptable' works as an abstracted idea of acceptability, rather than a specific way of predicting how commonly a particular social arrangement of power and rewards might be evaluated.

The best known deontologist, Kant, held that an ethical good action is done for the sake of duty, and is founded on reason alone, so what we *happen* to want is not relevant to the issue. So the form in which ethical conclusions of practical reason present to us differs from other kinds of conclusions. The form of the latter, Kant claims, is *hypothetical*:

If you want to achieve a certain end, then do what will bring this about.

But an action founded on reason alone does not depend on wants, so the corresponding format for an ethical – pure – practical judgement is *categorical*:

Do what is right.

Kant held that there was only *one* categorical imperative. Confusingly he explained this in several different ways, but these come down to the idea that an action done out of duty is one where the reason would be the same for all human beings. In following duty we are treating it as if it is a law of our human (for Kant – rational) nature, and therefore we should never treat others just as things to be used: *they* are ends of action, because *their* (rational) ends are *our* (rational) ends.

---

[3]Rawls was talking about society in general, but in this discussion we present the argument as applicable also to distinct organisations.

The idea of always treating others as ends, not means, has interesting implications for an organisation. If we are to act ethically we must always accept the rationality of others as of equal value to our own. But often human beings are not employed for their thoughts, but for their skills and labour power – even technical experts are often employed to function as, effectively, intelligent machines. People are thus engaged in organisations to perform tasks, not to contribute their (pure) rationality, in other words they are being treated solely as means and not as ends. Whilst many people would see a failure to consult with workers as undesirable, the implication of Kant's views is that it is *immoral*.

On Kant's version of deontology, there is a clear test as to whether a principle can be ethically right – could it consistently apply to all other humans? On this test, a duty such as keeping one's promises is justified because if we all made promises and then broke them when it suited us, trust would break down and the practice of making promises would fall apart. And similarly, if we could not assume that others were being honest with us then communication itself would cease, at least as a means of transmitting information. One might consider that modern litigation has made a step in that direction, when often employees are prevented from telling the truth, say to complaining customers, in case this prejudices a future court case.

This is not without its problems, though. An extremist acting out of their own weird sense of 'duty' that they would want everyone else to follow, would on this view still be acting morally. And it would seem that someone who acted at one moment on one universal principle and then at another time adopted another conflicting principle, is still acting out of duty, even though we might regard them as inconsistent over time.

A further issue is that in practice it is rare for someone to act completely out of a sense of duty without any regard for the consequences. We do sometimes feel justified in violating our principles for the sake of a certain balance of consequences. The most obvious example of this is the harmless lie to protect someone's feelings. Kant felt that duties could not conflict, but our day-to-day experience seems to indicate that our *values* do.

In summary, although the idea of duty irrespective of consequences is a plausible aspect of our ethical thinking, deontological theories of ethics do not capture all our ethical intuitions.

THE FOCUS ON AGENTS

8.7 The final theory of ethics that we will consider looks not at acts or their consequences, but rather at the idea of a good person. The question of what to do becomes what would a right-thinking or good person do? The focus is on what makes someone right-thinking, to which the basic answer is: the character traits or virtues that lead them to act ethically.

Virtue ethics in modern times has become popular as a resolution of the shortcomings of both deontology and consequentialism. Both Aristotle and Confucius identified a range of traits that would contribute towards right action: courage, benevolence, prudence and so on. Calling these 'virtues' implies that they are more than a predisposition always to, say, tell the truth; one might do that out of fear. Rather a virtuous person tells the truth because they value honesty. In this respect, there are linkages with deontological theories of morality.

What identifies something as a virtue, however? One common answer, deriving from Aristotle's use of the term 'eudaimonia'[4] is that they contribute to *human well-being*. This reveals the links that virtue ethics has with rule-based consequentialism – that certain rules, if followed consistently, would lead to positive results. On the virtue-ethical view, prudence, benevolence etc. lead to what we might call *the good life*. This implicitly judges that certain lives are good examples of well-being or flourishing. Well-being is thus more than just the kind of life that someone *chooses* to lead – on this view, some kinds of life are superior. Sensual indulgence, for example, may be enjoyable but is on this view inferior to a life in which there is some element of restraint. However, there is an element of subjectivity about what kind of life is to be preferred: Aristotle's preference for a life of reflection may not be to the taste of an agricultural worker, for whom virtues such as determination, or a love of nature, may be more important than, say, the love of truth.

In Aristotle's as well as Confucius' view of virtue ethics, there is also an emphasis on having the right *mean* of a quality. Someone demonstrating practical wisdom ensures that their virtuous behaviour is not taken to excess. Kindness is giving people the right amount of consideration – too much is indulgence, and too little is harshness.

Are there specific *organisational* virtues? The immediate candidate for this is leadership, which we stayed away from in Chapter 2, focusing instead on the definition of *leading*. We could consider leadership as a *composite* virtue, comprising judgement, practical wisdom, prudence, humanity and intellectual virtues such as a determination to get to the truth. This illustrates another aspect of virtue ethics – the 'unity' of the virtues: prudence, say, is no virtue if it is executed inhumanely. A further organisational implication of virtue ethics is that enhancing the ethical aspects of a firm's operations lies in developing several elements, and indicating how these are integrated in virtuous action.

As with the other ethical theories, there are shortcomings. Even when expressed as the question 'what would a virtuous person do?' virtue ethics does not guarantee that an action will be morally right. Connected with this is the problem of conflicts of virtues – when is it right to over-ride honesty on the

---

[4]Variously translated as 'happiness' 'flourishing' or 'well being' – one key aspect being that this is not a transitory moment of joy but a persisting long-term state.

basis of kindness, for example? In such situations, each option that one considers in effect is a decision to give greater weight to one virtue at the expense of another. To say that there should always be a suitable mean that can be identified that would sidestep such conflicts is an article of faith that cannot be easily justified. And how far is there consensus on which character traits are virtues, given that standards vary between different cultures?

PUTTING THEORIES OF ETHICS TOGETHER

8.8 Faced with three different ways to formulate ethical theories, and with the fact that each has its shortcomings, what value do these views have for organisations and managers? As noted earlier, it is invalid to simply treat these theories as tools such that if one does not 'work' – in the sense of justifying a particular course of action – then we will try another instead. These theories are alternative views of what is the case, and we cannot choose what is true or not, despite the absence of arguments that rule decisively in favour of one approach rather than another.

The uncertainty surrounding these approaches means that agents in a business setting may well seek to find the reinforcement of one argument by another – an action that is justified by more than one theory might be seen as more credible than one based on just one approach. It could be held that consequentialism, deontology and virtue ethics are all *approximations* to the essence of morality, so that a combination of all three might somehow capture the 'correct' parts of each theory. However, it is as likely that such a double level of approximation captures not the correct elements but the incorrect ones in a theory. So this does not necessarily move us closer towards what is ethically right.

But there is more to be said on this issue. In the discussion of virtue ethics it was explicitly noted that there are points where the approach seems to link with, in one place consequentialism, in another deontology. Similarly, even with the most out-and-out consequentialist theory, there is an ultimate source of good that is itself not justified by outcomes, but is valued in its own right. And finally, a 'duty' which produced no outcomes that were ethically relevant would not be accounted a duty at all.

What this seems to suggest is that morality may not be the simple concept we assume it is, but a composite of how we value outcomes, individual choices, and the character of agents. Perhaps we could express this composite nature of morality as follows:

a morally right action is one taken by an individual, prompted by a virtuous aspect of their character, within the constraints of what they perceive as non-negotiable aspects of the situation, and seeking to achieve the best overall outcomes.

Whether this provides any better test of what someone should do in a business, or other, context, is not clear. At least it does provide an indication of how different theories can be used in practice, without falling into the 'pick and choose' error mentioned earlier.

We have considered only a selection of ethical theories. More recent theoretical approaches to ethics, such as the 'ethics of care', or 'discourse ethics', address this question in different ways: the former by identifying specific values that counter a 'macho' style competitive ideology that pervades much western business, and the latter by focusing on how we arrive at ethical agreements. These are not discussed here, not because they have no value, but because they do not address the fundamental question of how an individual decides what they should do.

In conclusion then, in this chapter we have seen how the three major categories of ethical theory each focus on one aspect of the process of acting ethically. Ethical thinking, however, seems to require some attention to be given to all three aspects.

In the next, and final chapter, we shall look at more corporate aspects of the question of the goodness of business.

QUESTIONS FOR CONSOLIDATION

1 How would the three different ethical theories deal with the issues of cultural diversity that we discussed in Chapter 6?

2 Albert Carr once famously argued that lying is sometimes essential in business negotiations. Could this ever be justified on a virtue-ethical basis?

3 How should a manager approach a situation where two members of staff disagreed, where one was arguing from a consequentialist perspective and the other from a virtue perspective?

FURTHER READING

Aristotle (2004) *Nicomachean Ethics,* ed. J. Barnes and J. Thompson. Penguin Classics.

Habermas, J. (1995) *Justification and Application: Remarks on Discourse Ethics.* Polity Press.

Hume, D. (2011 [1740]) *A Treatise of Human Nature,* Book 3, ed. D. Norton and M. Norton. Oxford University Press.

Kant, I. (2012 [1775]) *Groundwork of the Metaphysic of Morals*, trans. C. Korsgaard, M. Gregor and J. Timmermann. Cambridge University Press.

Smart, J. J. C. and Williams, B. (1973) *Utilitarianism: For and Against.* Cambridge University Press.

BUSINESS AND SOCIETY

In this final chapter we will look at right and wrong as they relate to corporate activities, as distinct from the individual focus of the previous chapter.

When you have finished this chapter you will be able to:

- critically evaluate theories of corporate legitimacy
- analyse concepts of corporate responsibility
- identify and evaluate models of corporate engagement with social issues.

BUSINESS AND GOVERNMENT

9.1 What legitimises business? To answer this, we need first to consider the role of government. Whilst one might construe this issue as how governments manage relationships with those organisations that operate in their countries, in the modern era not only supersize firms such as Tata or BP, but also many other companies, operate across borders. These companies can move their operations swiftly between nation states, and thus by threatening to do this they can influence government policies, negotiate favourable deals with local suppliers, drive wages down, and so on. Add to this the interest of some industrialists in owning and/or controlling news media and other opinion-forming mechanisms, and the influence of business over government can look substantial.

Faced with this some have argued that the modern democratic state is declining in power in comparison with the largest multinationals.[1] Even before the contemporary increase in the scale of global trading, business in many countries has not always been entirely 'subject' to government. Many acts of legislation in past times have been direct responses to business lobbying, for example to cut taxation in order to stimulate more trade. The current issue is the ease with which corporations can move investment and operations across borders.

---

[1]See, for example Noreena Hertz, *The Silent Takeover: Global Capitalism and the Death of Democracy* (Arrow Books, 2002).

This changes the question of how business relates to government. Hitherto the key question was 'how is business subject to government?' and answers would refer to concepts such as social contracts, or regulatory frameworks. But the question might now be better phrased as 'how do business and government interact?', explicitly recognising that for the largest multinationals it is no longer a matter of subjection.

This power relationship is not as simple as government vis-à-vis big business. There is a complex of power structures, including global businesses, government collectivities (global industry agreements, economic blocs such as the European Union) and to a limited extent organised labour in the form of trade unions. This inter-relationship of different institutions creates a network of power structures, in which each party (institution) adjusts the spaces they occupy vis-à-vis other parties in response to changes in the sources and exercise of their power.

Nevertheless the largest businesses, in virtue of their size, market penetration and trading volumes, have increased their influence in this network. This means that they are less 'subjects' of government but better seen as *partners*. This is given greater credence when it is noted that in early 2012 the computing giant Apple had more cash reserves than even the United States government.

However, although the largest companies may have sufficient financial muscle to persuade even large governments to modify or even reverse policies, there is an asymmetry about their respective positions. Governments, even ones that are not popular, generally have the right to enforce their wishes on a population, by more or less coercive means if necessary. While a company can use certain mechanisms to influence government policy it cannot *force* changes. Its strongest 'card' is its ability to undermine that country's economy.

One important impact of the growth of corporate power is on the 'rule of law' – the principle that all in a country are subject to, and should obey, the laws of that country. This is built in to certain models of CSR, such as that developed by Archie Carroll,[2] which identifies obedience to the law as one of the basic imperatives for a corporation. However, the network of power relationships discussed above undermines the authority of this principle. As noted above, a business can simply avoid being subject to one legislative framework by moving its operations to another country with less stringent requirements. Whilst this is not easily done, for there are extensive costs incurred with such switching, it still remains an option for a company that becomes more attractive the more demanding the legislation involved.

Also, although law is a mechanism for implementing political ends, it is not an *automatic* mechanism. Laws are only as good as the processes – and motives – for their enforcement. Many laws are not enforced for various reasons; a law

---

[2] A. B. Carroll (1979) 'A three-dimensional conceptual model of corporate social performance', *Academy of Management Review*, 4: 497–505.

may have become outdated or a key power group has threatened reprisals if the government chooses to implement a certain law. The key point here is that enforcement of law is a *choice*, and for certain purposes it may not be exercised.

CORPORATE LEGITIMACY

9.2 Notwithstanding the preceding discussion, the question remains as to what right a company has to carry on its business.

One answer is that a corporation has this right because of the benefits it brings to society, such as employment, goods and services and tax revenues. Against this consequentialist argument we might set the range of environmental damage to the natural world, and the stresses that employment sometimes brings to workers. We might also question the benefits of some goods and services that businesses provide us with – to take the most obvious example, there is no doubt that smoking cigarettes is bad for people's health, and yet the tobacco industry thrives in almost all countries.

We might add that this argument is ambiguous between what legitimises business in general, and what would legitimise an individual company. For in the latter case, we could add a further objection that often the success of one business comes at the expense of competitors, so that the total benefit to the population at large might be a zero or near-zero sum outcome.

The significant outcomes of business can obscure other, more deontological arguments for its legitimacy. For example, the activity of working to support oneself and others provides life with a meaning and dignity that it lacks if all one's needs are provided for. One practical difficulty however with this is that much work is not designed to bring out its dignity, but is structured for efficiency only, and thus can often subtract the ennobling aspects of tasks as these may be unprofitable. But this does not negate the principle, only its application.

Other deontological arguments also undermine the idea that corporations are legitimised by the benefits they bring. Consumerism, for example, may be criticised as leading to a society where many things we produce are unnecessary for a fulfilling life, and can positively detract from this. As we have seen, from a non-western perspective, the consumer society can also alienate us from the natural world.

There are alternative conceptions of what legitimises corporate activity. One view is that we treat the activity of organisations *on a parallel* with that of nations, at least conceptually. Laszlo Zsolnai suggests that principles used to justify nations going to war could be applied to corporations[3] – on this view, a company is legitimised if its activities in themselves are substantively

[3]L. Zsolnai 'Corporate Legitimacy', in *Business Ethics and Corporate Sustainability*, eds. Antonio Tencati and Francesco Perrini (Edward Elgar, 2011).

right, if the way it operates is procedurally fair, and if it brings positive and equitable benefits to all its stakeholders. Note that this is explicitly about particular businesses – not about 'business' as a whole.

Another way of looking at organisational legitimacy is to consider how far the organisation engages with society in order to establish the key needs of the community and how the production of goods or services can address these.[4] This discourse-ethical approach rejects the market justification that corporations are legitimated by the fact of their success. The deliberative approach requires businesses to demonstrate that what they do is a positive benefit across society. No matter that many of us on occasion buy hamburgers from fast food outlets – are we convinced that this is a suitable source of sustenance?

Both of these alternatives explain corporate legitimacy in relation to society. However, in both cases one might ask – which 'society'? A corporate entity that brings great benefits, fairly distributed, and engaged with its stakeholders in an affluent western country, might not be so when viewed from the perspective of citizens of some underdeveloped countries. Can we say that the 'societal' perspective here must mean the citizenship of the whole world? Perhaps, but then issues such as the process of engagement become prohibitively difficult to administer, and exactly what counts as procedurally fair is viewed differently in different cultures. So neither of these approaches is operable in practice – not that this refutes them, but it does mean that on their own they cannot function as tools to test out the legitimacy of any business.

A more radical, libertarian response might be simply to ask whether business requires a justification at all. If an individual business produces more good than bad, or even is ethically neutral, is that not enough? Do not businesses, and entrepreneurs, have the *right* to do whatever is permitted by the law, so long as it is not in itself immoral?

The idea clearly only applies to for-profit bodies, not governmental or charitable ones. The claim that a business has a *right* is not clear. The features of human beings that justify their rights do not apply to corporations – dignity, human flourishing, pleasure and pain do not make sense when applied to organisations. Of course they do apply to *individual entrepreneurs*, but that does not give corporations legitimacy, only those people who get them started. It is true that a company is generally free to do anything that the law allows, but that is a tautology – in this case 'free' simply means *allowed by law*: this goes no way at all to justifying what companies do. If on the other hand 'free' means *morally* free, then this becomes the claim that a company is morally justified to do whatever the law allows it to do, but this cannot be

[4]One way of looking at this is provided in Guido Palazzo and Andreas Georg Scherer (2006) 'Corporate Legitimacy as Deliberation: A Communicative Framework', *Journal of Business Ethics*, 66: 71–88.

defended. For example, it is *legally* acceptable in many countries for majority shareholders of a company to sell company assets and take the proceeds of the sale as dividends, not ploughing anything back into the firm – but this is not ethically defensible.

RIGHTS

9.3 Whilst corporations may not have rights, *human* rights have an acute relevance for corporations, as these often constrain business activity. What makes something a human, or perhaps we might say 'natural', right is contentious – it could be argued that a 'right' is only something that is defined legally. But in general the idea seems to be respected, if not always honoured, in practice. Although it is common to distinguish between positive rights (that contribute to well-being) and negative ones (that protect us from ill-treatment) there is also an argument that all rights have to be respected simultaneously. We might add to these that human rights cannot be negated by other considerations.[5] Also we are justified in pressing for our rights to be respected, though *how* we press for these is itself subject to moral considerations: in a corporate context at least, I cannot justify extreme violence simply because it is an effective means to secure my rights.

Amartya Sen has added an important extra element to the notion of human rights – *debatability*. What this implies is that since we live very diverse lives, with different needs, affiliations and interests, the manner in which these link with our humanity (and thereby our fundamental natural human rights) requires processes of reconciliation, to ensure that our humanity is preserved even when superficial cultural features appear to be incompatible. Hence human rights need to be a subject of public deliberation and discussion.[6]

What exactly is a human right, though? Different theories have been advanced. One is that they are based on some kind of 'natural law', another that they derive from nothing other than the fact that we are human. Another is that human rights are those standards that are common across cultures. In a further view, John Rawls has argued that human rights are derived from the nature of a *people* as being either 'liberal' or 'decent'; underlying these idealised terms is the idea that rights exist within any society that meets certain preconditions of a reasonably tolerable life.

All of these views stand at some distance from the level of the corporation, as they are primarily concerned with the idea of the individual in society. A corporation or organisation is a part of what sustains society, indeed the network of organised economic activity is virtually by definition

---

[5]Though they might be over-ruled.

[6]A. Sen, 'Elements of a theory of human rights', *Philosophy and Public Affairs* (2004).

what enables a society to exist at all. So the responsibilities of a society to respect human rights devolve also to any organisation that operates within that society. Human rights thus imply an imperative for a corporation to respect them. The fact that often things generally regarded as a human right are violated does not negate the principle – it just shows that corporations are not always just.

What is more of a challenge is the argument that in some cases commercial imperatives can, in principle, over-ride human rights. When might this happen? Many organisations handle sensitive information and thus have rules about confidentiality. One channel of communication that could be a source of leaks is email. Also an organisation can be liable for improper or illegal email messages sent out by its employees. As a result, many companies occasionally screen the email traffic of their workforce to check that what is sent out respects company rules, is decent, legal etc. It could be argued that in doing so they violate the right to privacy.

That law in many countries allows organisations to do this, is not a demonstration of its validity – law is not a good indicator of morality. But one interesting feature of some legal systems is the idea of *proportionality*. This is the idea that whilst an organisation may have *some* right to read staff emails, it does not have an *absolute* right to do so on any occasion. The principle of proportionality implies that the organisation is justified to do this only in proportion to the level of threat to its security. So the organisation could legitimately vet the emails of certain people frequently, perhaps because they deal with especially sensitive information, but the checking of trusted employees with lower levels of access to information is only justified if done more rarely. Proportionality might also imply that some random checking is acceptable – how much is again dependent on the sensitivity of the information and the likelihood of it leaking. But the principle makes clear that a blanket practice of reading all emails of staff is not justified.

This might therefore act as a basis for justifying violations of human rights to avert threats to an organisation – that such violations may be acceptable in proportion to the importance and scale of the risk presented. However, this may be insufficient. For example, in the context of the behaviour of *governments*, deontological considerations have been deployed to undermine this view: even when it is accepted that a particular individual might have information that could be used by a government to avert a major terrorist attack, torture is not generally deemed ethically acceptable. This, however, is not quite as straightforward a point as it might seem – such an argument only implies that *extreme* violations of human rights are unjustified. Given that in a corporate context the most extreme event that we encounter is dismissal, it could be said that these lower-level violations of human rights by organisations can be justified in proportion to the risk of the negative consequences that they avoid. Perhaps if the company building starts falling down then it is acceptable to do whatever it takes to save lives, and the question of, say, personal privacy is irrelevant in such a context.

But there are still objections to this position. There is the view that violations of human rights happen not because they are necessary but because an individual cannot think of how to get the same outcome without such violation. On this view, the company reading staff emails has failed to be sufficiently innovative to protect its data without invading privacy. However, this seems to make the question of the inviolability of an individual's rights depend on the factual question of whether or not there is an alternative that will both achieve the corporation's ends and still respect human rights – unless of course it is alleged that there is always an alternative that will do this, which looks like an article of faith.

Overall then, the idea of human rights seems to provide an ethical imperative for corporations to respect these. It remains unclear as to how far these *have* to be respected, however. Examples seem to indicate that there are cases where human rights may be violated, but it is not clear how far this can go.

RESPONSIBILITY

9.4 A key phrase in the question of organisations and the good is *corporate social responsibility*. This has become so prevalent that in some quarters it has subsumed the older term 'business ethics' even though the two have distinct meanings. It has also spawned related concepts such as the 'corporate citizen'.

'Responsibility' is ambiguous. It can mean the attribution of causality – who or what made something happen. Or it can mean the imperatives that apply to an agent; someone's responsibility is to ensure that a certain project does not exceed its budget. The two senses are related: someone cannot have a responsibility to do something unless they can be held to be responsible for it coming about, in the sense of being part of the causal process that makes it happen. This has often been expressed as the idea that '*ought implies can*', which is reflected in our instinct that if something is not under a corporation's control then they are not liable for what happens. If a train is delayed because there is a tree fallen onto the line, then, although frustrating, this is not the fault of the train operating company.[7]

Now, responsibility in this sense of attribution of causality is not simply that one event caused another. As we saw in an earlier chapter, blame follows

---

[7]On various assumptions – such as that they were not responsible for cutting down trees in the vicinity of the line, and that they did not have suitable alternative routes that could be taken.

from an event being an *action*, freely chosen. A mere involuntary movement does not attract blame, and we are not responsible for its consequences – my slipping on an unseen banana skin does not make me responsible for the flower stall being knocked over. But I *am* responsible if my slipping is due to my sending a text message whilst I am walking along. Analogously, 'corporate responsibility' means that something is attributable to the company, not simply that the company happened to have caused certain outcomes.

What could it mean to say that a corporation 'accidentally' caused something? In the case of an individual, there are several reasons why we might dismiss what happened as being not their full responsibility: it was an involuntary movement, or someone was ill and this clouded their judgement, or they were mistaken about certain facts, and so on. But such excuses do not apply to an organisation. If a firm embarks on a joint venture and it later transpires that they did not have all the relevant information, they are not thereby *excused* from responsibility if something goes wrong. Similarly, if the machinery of a company unexpectedly malfunctions and emits noxious gases then that company is not excused from being responsible for the emission – even though the event in question could not have reasonably been foreseen.[8] These examples suggest that the language of action and responsibility is not applicable to organisations: a crucial part of that language of action is not just how we describe intentional actions, but also how we explain events which are *not* intentional, despite causality being present.

However, considering the same example of a company releasing poisonous gases into the atmosphere, suppose that a hurricane had damaged the company's systems, could we then say that the company did not release the gases, but the gases were released accidentally? Whilst legally there might remain the question of whether the company had sufficient back-up systems to minimise the damage, in principle it is possible that the company did everything reasonable to ensure that the gases would not be released, but the hurricane was beyond what could have been expected, so here the company was not responsible for the release. This argument would depict the situation analogously to an individual slipping in the street on a banana skin – an event that was not reasonably foreseeable and over which the agent has no control caused the events that led to the undesired outcome. Therefore, so this counter-example runs, if the language of excusing and mitigation can apply to a company, at least in some circumstances, then it is fair to say that companies and other organisations can be regarded as agents, and thus responsible for the outcomes of their actions.

Natural though this sounds, it is still not sufficient. In the case of an individual slipping in the street, we say that *I slipped*, but that there were reasons why I was not to blame. In the case of a factory exploding and

---

[8]Though in this case it is conceivable that some legal systems would not hold the company liable for such damage as may be caused.

releasing poison gas into the atmosphere, it is not that the company released the gas, but that the gas was released by equipment that the company owns. The point here is that a human agent is an identifiable entity to which both causation and blame is either attributed or excused. In the case of a company there is no single point of causation – there are members of the board, there are individual employees or teams of employees, there are various parts of the operation, any of which might be a contributory cause of a series of events such as the release of gas. And when such events occur we do not attribute blame to the company – we attribute *causality* to the collective operations of the company, but *blame* is reserved for individuals. Even though there are legal fictions such as the idea of 'corporate manslaughter' the blame for such acts falls on individuals – the directors, or those employees who carried out the acts in question.

But there is yet a further response someone might make here – if we cannot say that a company accidentally did something, then how can we say that it *deliberately* does anything, and in that case what sense can we make of that very natural way of speaking, that, say, EDF produces electricity? In other words, if corporations are not agents how come we can and do say that this company produces electricity, that one makes laptops and so on. However, whilst this objection demonstrates that grammatically we can use subject terms and action verbs with corporations, it does *not* demonstrate that responsibility attaches to corporations – after all, we talk of inanimate objects 'doing' things without that implying that we regard them as agents. The river broke its banks – but that does not mean that the river has intentions. In the case of a firm there are intentions, but they are the intentions of those individuals who contribute to what happens – shareholders, directors, employees etc.

There are important practical implications to this. One motive for some countries defining a concept of 'corporate manslaughter' is to pin down responsibility in complex situations. *The Herald of Free Enterprise* was a car ferry that sank in Zeebrugge harbour in 1987, killing nearly 200 passengers and crew. In the subsequent inquest it became clear that there was a whole catalogue of errors, individually small, but collectively sufficient to lead to the disaster. However, despite the acknowledged negligence on the part of many people, no criminal convictions were secured because the judge in a subsequent trial of the key individuals held that there was no single 'controlling mind' to whom responsibility could be attributed. The needs of legal systems to find a single point of complete responsibility are not consonant with the complexity of modern organised activity, where often many micro events combine to produce a macro outcome. The true attribution of responsibility in such a case should be proportionately divided amongst a number of human agents, from the Chief Executive down to the relevant members of the crew. This is generally too difficult to establish in most cases, which is why it is not practicable from a legal point of view. But legal practicalities aside, if a series of actions by a number of different people collectively leads to a certain outcome, then in principle each of those agents shares the responsibility for what happens.

The idea of corporate responsibility assumes that corporations can be agents, and thus responsible for the events that their operations cause. We have seen that in the case of human agency, which is the model on which our understanding of responsibility is built, if there is the possibility of intention for which one is responsible, there must also be the possibility of unintended action, and also of action for which one is excused responsibility. These concepts do not work with the idea of an organisation. So although we do elliptically talk of corporations 'doing' things, this is not an attribution of agency but only of causality.

'SOCIAL' RESPONSIBILITY

9.5 The other side to CSR is the meaning of 'social'. This takes the sense of 'responsibility' in which it implies a moral imperative – so that we act 'responsibly' when we fulfil a moral imperative, and thus by extension we can apply the same terminology to organisations.[9]

One striking feature of modern corporate social responsibility initiatives is the selectivity with which organisations identify which social obligations they will fulfil. Philosophically, however, all obligations that apply to an organisation should be taken into account in their policies. From such an all-inclusive perspective, it might seem that *no* organisation is 'fully' responsible, since probably none can meet all of its obligations. This is too strong a claim though. One might as well argue that on a parallel basis no individual human being is good, because we all at some point fail to fulfil some obligation or other. But clearly notwithstanding their occasional failings, we do identify some people as good. So it may be that what counts as 'responsible' in this context is not the same as fulfilling every possible obligation.

Faced with this, an organisation might go to an opposite position, and assert that so long as *some* obligation is being fulfilled then it can be said to act responsibly. So a company that sponsors sports events, for example, may claim that this *is* their CSR strategy, as if a collection of such activities is sufficient to demonstrate the fulfilment of their ethical duties. However, this is also inadequate. It may be difficult to specify how far all the duties of a corporation have been addressed. But if a certain imperative has not been addressed, that cannot simply be erased from consideration because some other imperatives have been addressed instead. There needs to be

---

[9]The following discussion does use the language of action and responsibility in the context of corporations, but this is intended elliptically, and not as a negation of the argument of the previous section.

some kind of account that explains how the full range of imperatives is approached, and why some are addressed and others less so (if at all).

One can identify different aspects of CSR initiatives, arising from different ethical theories:

- the corporate contributor, that aims to ensure that on balance more good is done than bad as a result of their operations
- the corporate citizen, that aims to act in a manner that could be emulated by, or even provide the model for, other organisations
- the virtuous company, that aims to treat stakeholders fairly, humanely, with respect, and to honour justice and rights.

The corporate contributor

The idea of a corporate 'contributor' is that the outcomes of the organisation's activities are evaluated on a consequentialist basis. So a firm is *assayed*, in effect, for the total benefit of its operations against the total drawbacks. One might therefore look to positive outcomes (such as the provision of jobs for employees, returns made to shareholders, charitable donations, the benefits of the company's products and services) and set these against negative ones (consumption of natural resources, loss of jobs in competitor firms, destruction of local environments, depletion of local economic variety).

But in practical terms there are shortcomings with this process. For one thing, there is the difficulty of comparing different kinds of outcome: how much destruction of the rain forest can equate to the payment of good salaries to employees (a benefit to them if no one else)? Also the adoption of consequentialist reasoning can often lead a corporation to develop a policy of *compensation*. Consider a bank that draws substantial profits out of its savings and loans operations (and thus takes value out of its customers' pockets and puts it into those of its shareholders). Does it offset this by having a community policy that benefits local schools, for example? At issue here is that compensation implies that the disbenefits of the operation of the organisation are not addressed – instead something else is offered as a counter-balance. Arguably this is virtually a bribe to the community to tolerate poor business practice.

In addition, more obviously than with individual action, is the issue of how widely do we measure relevant outcomes? Consider a firm such as Microsoft, which produces (amongst other things) computer operating systems that then are used by others for many purposes. How far is the success (or failure) of those different uses of the operating system an outcome of the work of Microsoft? It might be alleged that in a small part they are: without Microsoft's operating systems for PCs we might never have had such widespread use of internet browsers, say, and the resulting access to a vast range of other internet based applications. On this argument, then, we could say that to some extent at least, one component of the total benefits of Microsoft's activities is the opportunity for others to build on Microsoft services, to develop further positive services.

However, if Microsoft gets some credit for the positive things that people can do with the company's operating system, does this imply that it also gets some of the blame when a third party does something unethical using that operating system? If someone develops a program that runs on Microsoft based systems and raids people's bank accounts, we would not blame the company for this, but the perpetrator of the theft. But if there is no blame for the bad things that happen then on a parallel basis there should be no credit for the good things.

On the other hand, consider a TV company that produces a documentary highlighting the difficulties of a disadvantaged section of the population. Suppose also that subsequent to the programme being aired, charitable donations to help those with this disadvantage increase. Does not this causal linkage suggest some degree of credit? And equally, would not some degree of blame ensue if the programme instead highlighted problems caused by that group and immediately afterwards there was a drop in the levels of donations?

The idea of a corporate contributor is difficult to establish with precision, and the extent to which attribution of causality justifies attribution of responsibility makes it problematic to apply.

The corporate citizen

The concept of the 'corporate citizen' has become a popular alternative approach to CSR, although in this discussion the phrase is used in a slightly different way from its usual interpretation. The idea of a firm as a *citizen* attempts to build a more positive construction on the 'legal person' fiction. It implies that there are duties that people or entities have simply because of their 'citizenship' status. In effect then such duties apply irrespective of other features of a situation, giving this something of a Kantian ring. However, the use of the same term for both individuals and for corporations has a deeper nuance, that corporations should interact with the community in parallel with how individuals do.

The idea of a citizen is that they *participate* in society, contributing to the community over and above their legal obligations. So a corporate citizen is one that makes a contribution over and above its legal obligations to shareholders. One interpretation of this is that corporations make their own charitable donations, but this is not a role, in the way that citizenship is – it could as much be done as a form of compensation as discussed above.

Another is that one's status as a citizen entitles one to participate in national decisions via voting and representation. Companies certainly do participate in national decisions, but often by the more dubious method of lobbying, which can often subvert the process of enacting the expressed wishes of a country's real citizens.

What seems to remain with the idea of a corporate citizen is not a great deal more than an obligation for a company to provide services to the community that go beyond their trading activities. There are doubtless issues of thresholds here – how much corporate giving counts as sufficient to entitle a firm to call itself a corporate citizen? And equally there are definitional questions – which activities count as giving back to the community, as opposed to those which might be seen as simply PR? But even when these practical matters are resolved it would seem that the most such activities can amount to is to denote a company as a corporate benefactor. Citizenship lies in a more complex and two-way relationship.

The virtuous organisation

This is the idea that an organisation might adopt a similar approach to what in an individual would be regarded as a virtuous character. One might first ask what is the closest analogue with 'character'?

Someone's character tells us what on the whole they are like, as friends or co-workers. It also helps us foresee their likely behaviour in different contexts – again only as a tendency, not as a prediction. We could look to the idea of the culture of an organisation as doing the same things for an organisation. Organisational culture is even defined sometimes as 'what it feels like to work around here' and some models of culture draw up categories that include likely responses to events.

As with virtue ethics in general this interpretation of CSR takes the emphasis off specific events and looks rather more broadly at policies and patterns of events. In practice it is unlikely that this would be the sole source of an organisation's approach to CSR – it can look more like a vision than a formal policy. Nevertheless strains of virtue may be found in many aspects of corporate practice. The focus on equality in the workplace is one example, even though this may have been less an expression of virtue and more just legal compliance. Other examples of virtue-like policy in organisations are expressions of honest dealing, fairness, respect for others. And just as there are sometimes gaps between what individuals claim and what they actually do, so with organisations there are gaps between formal statements of value and organisational reality.

One issue that was not discussed with individual virtue ethics is what we mean by 'character'. The term suggests some feature of a person that is relatively stable – tending to persist over a period of months rather than days. This implies that moral character is slow to change. But if we draw someone's attention to a certain value today, we will not excuse them tomorrow by saying that they have not had time to change: virtue ethics does not erase the responsibility, blame and reward for actions. And similar points could be made of organisational culture. It is partly for this reason that some have tended to differentiate virtue ethics from the deontological-consequential divide, and claim that it may be compatible with one or even both of those approaches. There are however differences between how we judge individual actions and organisational ones in virtue terms. If someone of known good character lapses and does something, say unkind or dishonest – as all humans lapse occasionally – then whilst we do not erase the wrongdoing, it is often moderated by our knowledge that it is a one-off. So when a person who is generally prudent does something rash, that is regarded as an aberration. Equally, if someone is thought of as being of bad character then in similar fashion we tend to take this into account in judging them – a certain act of unkindness is seen not as an isolated episode but as a manifestation of a general ill will towards others, for example. The point is that our view of someone's level of virtue affects our view of their actions. Their character colours their actions.

Can we say the same of an organisation? Suppose an organisation is known to have a supportive culture where employees are developed, rewarded for good performance, and generally treated well. Then an employee makes a mistake and gets swiftly fired. Whilst we might be surprised at this, for it conflicts with our prediction of how the firm might have reacted, we do not diminish the event because of the culture of the firm. It is no less harsh a response. The action is not changed in our perception by the kind of organisation that does it, unlike our view of human acts. This comes back to earlier arguments, that whilst we can talk about the organisation doing something, the deeper ramifications of what an action is are not applicable. Similarly the deeper ramifications of character do not apply to organisations, even though we do talk about people's collective behaviour in terms of culture. So whilst it is convenient to use the language of virtue in assessing the approach to CSR taken by an organisation, it is unlikely to provide a complete basis for this.

Overall these categories indicate that the pretensions of 'corporate social responsibility' do not fit any ethical theory completely. Consequentialist views are perhaps the closest, but even these do not provide sufficient explanation of approaches to CSR .

At the end of this chapter then, we see the following:

- Modern businesses are not simply subject to regulation by individual governments.
- Businesses are not legitimised by an appeal to a general 'right' for them to carry on their activity unless restrained by the law.
- An organisation might in specific circumstances be justified in violating some human rights.
- Corporate entities are not agents and therefore cannot be regarded as the bearers of responsibility.
- Approaches to corporate social responsibility do not fit easily with any particular ethical theory.

QUESTIONS FOR CONSOLIDATION

1 A social enterprise is one that operates in the for-profit sector, but with a mission to achieve positive social aims, such as running conservation schemes. What potential drawbacks might there be to the argument that they are legitimised by their ethical mission?

2 In the text we saw that firms might on very specific occasions be justified in violating a human right. How far does this differ depending on whether the organisation in question is a state body, NGO, or private sector company?

FURTHER READING

Crane, A., Matten, D. and Spence, L. (2007) *Corporate Social Responsibility – Readings and Cases in a Global Context.* London: Routledge.

Freeman, M. (2011) *Human Rights (Key Concepts)* 2nd edn. Cambridge: Polity Press.

Randtorff, J. D. (2009) *Responsibility, Ethics and Legitimacy of Corporations.* Copenhagen: Business School Press.

CONCLUSION

On reviewing what has been written in this book, it is striking how much has not been said. There is a wealth of philosophical material that could have been employed – process philosophy for example, or existentialism, or the many renewed developments in recent decades of some of the ancient Asian philosophical traditions. Also there are many topics that have been hardly touched upon – wisdom, leadership, the nature of thought and its relationship with language, consciousness, to name just a few.

In defence of the coverage in this text, I might remind the reader of what was stated at the start: that this introduction to the field would not be a complete exploration of the philosophical 'space', but rather it would shine a light into some of the more important spaces. In doing this, the most valuable lesson that one might draw is what more needs to be considered. A few of the questions that merit greater exploration, in the light of the discussions in this book, are:

- What exactly do we mean when we talk in collective terms about an 'organisation'?
- Is there anything special about the thinking processes, and judgement, exercised in the managerial role?
- What, exactly, is 'knowledge' in organisations, and how does this relate to the 'intellectual' virtues?
- How far can we hope for general theories about how organisations work, or should we restrict ourselves to more narrowly focused or even organisation-specific ideas?
- How does freedom fit with the authority and control implicit in organisations?
- Is it even possible, in principle, for a company operating in a market environment to completely fulfil its 'social obligations'?

As indicated at the start, philosophising is not evaluated by the conclusions it reaches, but rather by the processes taken in order to reach them. It is not a search for answers, but rather an examination of the structure of our thinking and rationale that underpins the answers we already have. If after reading this you have questions about what an organisation is, what we know about it, or what can be said about how it 'acts', then even if you disagree profoundly with the answers given here, the job of this text is done.

GLOSSARY

Act utilitarianism   An ethical theory that holds the rightness or wrongness of an action is determined by its direct consequences. Contrasted with **rule utilitarianism.**

Alienation   The idea that a human being may be placed in a social context that inhibits the full expression of their true human nature.

Categorical Imperative   An ethical view of Immanuel Kant, that what is right is what represents a command of duty irrespective of personal desires. Formulated in several ways, but based on the idea that a principle of action, when ethically right, applies with equal import to all rational beings.

Cogito ergo sum   According to Descartes, the one thing that we can be sure of without doubting is that we think (translated from the Latin, the phrase means, I think therefore I am).

Coherentism   The idea that knowledge is best understood in terms of how its different elements fit together — how coherent is the whole body of knowledge.

Connotation   The elements of the sense of a term: what we understand by a term, as opposed to what things we actually judge are examples of that term. So the connotation of the term 'human being' would be what we think of when someone talks to us about being a human being — the ideas we have about what a human is. See also **denotation.**

Consequentialism   The ethical theory that what is right or wrong, ethically, is determined by the consequences of an action. Best known example of this is **utilitarianism.**

Critical theory   The project to liberate us from those assumptions that lock in social attitudes and prejudices, by critically examining and reflecting on their origins and influence in our thought. Associated with several European philosophers of the twentieth century, notably Jurgen Habermas.

Denotation   The totality of objects referred to by a term, contrasted with connotation. So the denotation of the term 'human being' is the totality of things that can be described in this way. The different ways in which connotation and denotation are seen to inter-relate form the bases of many theories of the meaning of a term.

Deontology   The conception of ethical rightness as lying in the nature of certain actions in themselves, rather than looking at the results or the personal traits of those who perform these. The best known, but by no means the only, example of deontology is Kant's idea of a categorical imperative.

Desire-belief model of action   The view that actions can be explained in terms of what someone desired or wanted, in the context of their beliefs. Often, though not necessarily, associated with the idea of action as the means to achieve desired ends.

Determinism   The claim that all our actions are fully explained in terms of their preceding causes. See also **free will**.

Discourse ethics   A conception of ethics developed by Habermas, which presents ethical norms as justified in so far as these are accepted communally via a process of dialogue.

Doctrine of the mean   Aristotle argued that virtuous behaviour was a mean between extremes of behaviour. There are some similarities with the teachings of Confucius.

Double hermeneutic   The idea of Giddens that the technical language of social science, and the ordinary language we use in day-to-day life, have a two-way relationship, so that each domain influences the other.

Dreamtime   The traditional world-view of native Australians, that combines ideas of myth with geographical orientation.

Emancipatory theory   See critical theory.

Empiricism   The emphasis on experience via our senses as the key source of our knowledge.

Essence   Stemming from Aristotle's theory of definition, the idea that something has a specific nature which captures what it basically is, such as (perhaps) having the desire to socialise with others as part of the essence of a human being. Contrasted with *accident* which would be a feature that something happens to have but not in virtue of what it actually is – say a particular colour of hair.

Eudaimonia   In ancient Greek, this meant something like 'human flourishing' and it was a central concept in the ethical views of Socrates, Plato and Aristotle. It is sometimes construed as 'happiness' but really quite a specific kind of happiness – that of leading a fulfilled life – is what is intended.

Expectancy or **valency theory**   A theory of motivation associated with Vroom and others (and similar to the **desire-belief model of action**) under which someone is motivated to do something in so far as they are attracted to it and they hold appropriate beliefs about how to achieve it.

Falsifiability   Popper held that a genuinely scientific theory should take risks – should not only explain what was the case, but also make predictions that had both the possibility of being confirmed and the possibility of being falsified. Theories that insulated themselves from the possibility of being refuted were, Popper argued, pseudo-science.

Family resemblance   Wittgenstein's conception that the different ways we use a term may have similarities without necessarily having a single underlying basis that justifies all and only the uses made of that term.

Foundationalism   The idea that knowledge should be based on sure foundations, and that the main job of the philosophical theory of knowledge is to find out what those foundations are and how we can build on them. Often contrasted with **coherentism**.

Free will   The view that humans can feely choose (at least some of) what they do, and that we are not forced by natural causes to act in given ways. Previously seen as the contrary of determinism.

Gettier examples   Counter-examples to the theory that knowledge is justified true belief, the first example being developed by Edmund Gettier. The counter-examples all are based on the idea that the 'justification' is interrupted and then restored, so that although the belief is true the individual is incorrect in relying on their 'justification' as warranting their belief.

'Great man' theory of leadership   The idea that leadership is best understood in terms of the qualities of great leaders of the past.

Guanxi   The Chinese idea that there should be a strong personal linkage between people before they can rely on each to do business together successfully.

Heuristic principles   Methods of resolving questions that are not logically water-tight, such as trial and error, rules of thumb, or approaches that work well in practice even though not supported by theory.

Hypothetico-deductivism   Popularised (but not invented) by Karl Popper, the idea that a scientific investigation proceeds by drawing out (deducing) observable consequences from the theory or hypothesis that then function as predictions of the theory, and then checking to see if these predictions come about.

Inductivism   View that a scientific theory is proved or disproved by the accretion of supporting data.

Infinite regress   A weakness of a position, that it can never be resolved to a fundamental conclusion, but either each step of justification can be further questioned (e.g. using a repeated 'why' technique) or the position itself gives rise to repeated iterations of the same idea without any basis for this terminating.

Inter-subjectivity   The phenomenon of generally agreed practices, beliefs or theories, which cannot be objectively justified, but are nevertheless accepted by all members of a given community.

Interpretavism   An approach to knowledge of social phenomena based on the idea that these cannot be objectively described, but always require interpretation by observers.

Justified true belief   The theory that knowledge needs not only to be true but also to have a sound justification. Originally propounded by Plato. See **Gettier examples**.

Knowing how and knowing that   The distinction between skills-based knowledge and knowledge of facts.

Master–slave relationship   Hegel's theory of human self-consciousness and inter-action, based on an idea of a struggle for domination.

Modernism   The belief in a steady upward trend of progress in science, and thereby in society generally. Based on a confidence in rational methods of enquiry and policy.

Moral luck   The phenomenon of an individual's ethical actions depending on chance events in the world, so that in one case driving a speeding car is just dangerous, and in another case the driver kills someone, and thus in the latter case becomes a killer, whilst in the first case they were just foolish – though the intentions and bodily movements in both cases were the same. Often given as an argument against ethical theories that rely solely on motive as the basis for rightness.

Nominal definition   The theory that definition is solely of words. Contrasted with **real definition**.

Normal science   Kuhn depicted scientific investigation as falling into two contrasting periods: 'normal' science when the main work of scientists was to elaborate on and solve puzzles created by the dominant paradigm explanation; and 'revolutionary' science when the paradigm itself was rejected and there was no commonly accepted guiding principle or model to direct investigation.

Noumena   Kant's term for things in themselves, about which we can have no direct knowledge (apart perhaps from our own sense of freedom). We experience things not as they are, but as they appear to us. See **phenomena**.

Ostensive definition   Defining something not by words, but by showing examples of it.

Ought-is question   The argument about whether evaluative statements (marked often by containing the word 'ought' or its cognates) can ever be derived logically from factual statements (i.e. statements of what is the case). Hume originated this way of expressing the argument, himself arguing strongly that an 'ought' cannot be derived from an 'is'.

Paradigm   Kuhn's term for the dominant model in a scientific discipline, that guides further research. A good example might be evolution in biology.

Phenomena   In Kant's use of the term, these were things as they presented themselves to us, and subject to certain principles of how we can experience them (e.g. as existing in space and time, and subject to causation). Contrasted with **noumena**.

Phronesis   Ancient Greek term used in particular by Aristotle, generally translated as 'practical wisdom' though sometimes also associated with prudence.

Positivism   The view that all knowledge is founded in what is observable – the term originated with August Comte, and is closely allied with empiricism.

Postmodernism   A cluster of attitudes towards knowledge and society, based on the view that modernism is unable to capture the full range of social phenomena or policy; postmodernism is sometimes loosely linked with critical theory.

Practical reason   Reasoning as applied to action. Deliberation about what to do. Aristotle and Kant in particular discussed quite distinct approaches to this concept.

Pseudo-science   Popper's term for theories that purported to be scientific, but did not fit his conception of falsifiability. He particularly singled out Marxism and psycho-analysis as examples.

Rationalism   Generally the belief in the use of reason to gain knowledge, but often applied specifically to the assumptions of certain European philosophers in the seventeenth and eighteenth centuries (especially Descartes, Leibniz and Spinoza) who believed that our knowledge of the world could be entirely gained via the use of reason.

Real definition   The idea that defining a term reveals its true, real nature, rather than just an indication of the use of words. Generally seen as the opposite of **nominal definition**.

Realism   The belief that our senses provide us with knowledge of a world that is independent of us, and of our perceptions, and that we can have a fairly accurate knowledge of what it is like.

Referential opacity   A statement where one term cannot be substituted by another with the same reference is said to be referentially opaque: for example suppose it is a fact that Francis Bacon wrote Shakespeare's plays – it still can be the case that some-one (who does not know this) might believe that the author of those plays was gay, and yet not believe this of Francis Bacon. In contrast, a statement that I shook the hand of the President of the USA (in 2012) says the same thing as one that says I shook the hand of Barak Obama – it is referentially transparent.

Relativism   The idea that all knowledge is relative to the culture or background of individuals or groups, and that therefore there is no basis for correcting the state-ments of someone from outside one's own cultural circle.

Revolutionary science   Kuhn's term for those periods when a scientific discipline lacks any overall guiding model or framework. A good example of this might be the state of physics just before Einstein proposed his theories of relativity.

Rigid designation   A term that refers to the same thing, even had the facts been different – so the term 'Henry Ford' refers to the same person no matter what might have actually happened (or it refers to no one) but the term 'The founder of Ford Motors', which actually refers to Henry Ford, could have been different, if someone else had set up that company. So 'Henry Ford' is a rigid designator, whilst 'Founder of Ford Motors' is not. This idea, developed by Saul Kripke, has been compared to Aristotle's idea of essence.

Rule Utilitarianism   A version of utilitarianism whereby it is not an individual action that is justified in terms of its results, but a general rule of behaviour. Some have argued that this is less a consequentialist view and rather more like a deonto-logical one.

Scepticism   The general doubt as to whether what we access through our senses provides us with knowledge of the external world – not in individual cases, but in general, of whether there is a world out there at all.

Servant leadership   A view of leadership that depicts it as a service to the team and other stakeholders.

Stipulative definition   A definition that fixes, intentionally, how a term is to be used. Often employed when there is no general agreement about the peripheral examples of the term.

Substance   In Aristotle's writings, the fundamental basis of all existence is a substance, though his explanation of this term is not unanimously agreed even today.

Transference (Freudian)   The idea that clients of a Freudian analyst will often transfer feelings, especially sublimated or repressed ones about their parents, on to the analyst.

Ubuntu   A view widely held in southern Africa, based on the idea that humans should be understood primarily in collective terms, rather than as individuals.

Utilitarianism   The most common version of consequentialism, stating that what is right is what produces the 'greatest good for the greatest number'.

Vertu   A term used by Machiavelli, denoting a certain form of enterprise or courage.

Virtue Ethics   The view that what is ethically right should not be sought in the act itself (deontology) or in its consequences (utilitarianism) but in the nature of those who act ethically – in their virtues; deriving from Aristotle and Confucius, the virtues that are cited in this context often include personal qualities such as prudence, humility, courage, honesty, integrity, charity.

GENERAL FURTHER READING

If you wish to read more on this subject, there are several different sources, depending on your interests.

If you want to know about philosophy in general:

Simon Blackburn, *Think,* Oxford University Press, 1999.

André Comte-Sponville, *The Little Book of Philosophy* (trans F. Wynne), Vintage Books, 2005.

Additionally, the online Stanford Encyclopedia of Philosophy is an invaluable and authoritative source for information on a whole range of philosophical ideas, and for the ideas of great philosophers of the past: http://plato.stanford.edu/

Some of the great works of the past are quite accessible – notably Plato's dialogues in general, but especially relevant are: *Protagoras, Meno, Republic, Theatetus*; Descartes' *Meditations* and his *Discourse on Method*, and J. S. Mill's *Utilitarianism*.

Of more modern texts:

Ludwig Wittgenstein's *Philosophical Investigations* is deceptive – easy to read individual paragraphs but the overall argument is more complex and more controversial than first sight might suggest.

Alisdair Macintyre's *After Virtue* (Duckworth, revised edition 2007) is a classic study in ethical theory.

If you want to explore more deeply the philosophy of management, there are a few books that are directly focused on this as a whole. A couple of titles that cover some aspects are:

Claes Gustafsson, *The Production of Seriousness: the Metaphysics of Economic Reason*, Palgrave, 2011.

Jos Kessels, Erik Boers and Pieter Mostert, *Free Space and Room to Reflect: Philosophy in Organisations*, Boom Publishers, 2004.

Campbell Jones and René Ten Bos, *Philosophy and Organisations*, Routledge, 2007.

Peter Koslowski, *Elements of a Philosophy of Management and Organization*, Springer, 2010.

However, the journal *Philosophy of Management*, as its name suggests, is solely concerned with this field, and may be accessed online:

http://www.libripublishing.co.uk/philosophy-of-management

Other journals such as the *Academy of Management Review*, *Organization*, or *Organisation Studies* also often run articles with a philosophical element to them.

NAMES INDEX

SUBJECT INDEX

ACKNOWLEDGEMENTS

All books are a composite, trying to build on ideas that come to one from many directions and from many sources. Amongst the innumerable sources that have inspired me and helped develop my ideas in this area must specifically be named the following:

My colleagues on the editorial board of the *Philosophy of Management* journal – Nigel Laurie, Ed Freeman, Frits Schipper, Mark Dibben and Wim Vandekerhove.

Colleagues at Middlesex University and University College London who may not have realised that discussions with them were contributing to my thinking on this subject and how and whether to teach this at undergraduate level – especially but by no means confined to Alan Durant, Nina Seppala, Alison Megeney, Richard Pettinger and Andrea Werner.

Other academic colleagues and teachers whose views (in some cases for quite some years) have influenced this writing of this book include Cristina Neesham, David Lutz, Michael Loughlin, Marja-Liisa Kakkuri-Kintilla, Pierre Guillet de Montoux, Jonathan Groucutt, James Wisdom, and Chris Cherry.

The many students who have participated in Philosophy of Management, Business Ethics, and Research Methods modules that I have delivered at several institutions, have contributed – far more than they may have realised – to the content that has found its way into this book.

There are very many others who also merit acknowledgement – too many to identify here.

To all of these I owe my gratitude for the time, space and stimulation to consider issues of philosophy in the organisational context. But of course the content here is entirely my own responsibility, mistakes, omissions, warts and all.

Lastly my great thanks to my wife, Lyn Thompson, for her support, as always with neither impatience nor deference, during the writing of this book.